BELAIR ACTIVE SCIENCE 2

Tony Laukaitis

Contents

Belair Publications

First published in 2001 by Belair Publications.
United Kingdom: Belair Publications, Apex Business Centre, Boscombe Road, Dunstable, LU5 4RL.

Editor: Hayley Willer
Layout artist: Suzanne Ward
Cover design: Martin Cross
Illustrations: Colin King

Every effort has been made to contact copyright holders of material used in this book. If any have been overlooked, we will be pleased to make any necessary arrangements.

British Library Cataloguing in Publication Data. A catalogue record for this book is available from the British Library.

ISBN 1 84191 071–6

Introduction

What is Active Science?

Active Science is a series of six books designed to be used with children aged five to eleven. The series provides teachers' notes and activity sheets matched to the topics in the QCA Scheme of Work for Science.

The activities are varied and challenging and encourage the children to think scientifically. The emphasis is on providing the children with first-hand experience of scientific practical work and investigation.

Active Science 2 can be used alongside the QCA Scheme as the basis of a year's work or it can be used to supplement existing schemes of work already in place in school.

The book is divided into eleven chapters. Each chapter consists of a teachers' page and three photocopiable activity sheets.

What is on the teachers' page?

- **Background** – This provides the necessary background knowledge for teachers to deliver the topic. This is not necessarily information that the children are required to know, but information to aid the teacher.
- **Activity pages** – This section contains:
  - the main learning objectives in terms of knowledge, understanding and skills, for each activity, to help teachers with planning and assessment
  - ideas for further activities
  - guidance points for discussion
  - safety warnings.
- **Oral work** – This section provides opportunities for:
  - discussion
  - questioning that encourages the children to think about the scientific process
  - oral presentations
  - inviting guest speakers into the classroom
  - role-play.
- **Written work** – This section provides ideas for written work, including:
  - comparing and contrasting
  - planning investigations
  - writing conclusions and explanations.
- **ICT** – A range of opportunities for the use of ICT in the Science Curriculum is provided, including:
  - researching information using CD-ROM and the Internet
  - using ICT programs to produce scientific information in the form of text and graphics
  - using computer databases
  - using data-handling packages to present results to experiments
  - using audiotapes and videotapes to record work.

What about the activity pages?

The photocopiable activity sheets contain a variety of activities that provide opportunities for the children to do the following.

- **Plan** – This includes:
  - asking and answering questions
  - making predictions
  - recognising when a test is unfair.
- **Obtain and present evidence** – This includes:
  - following simple instructions
  - making and recording simple observations and measurements
  - using simple apparatus
  - choosing methods of recording.
- **Consider evidence and evaluate** – This includes:
  - making simple comparisons
  - using results to draw conclusions
  - explaining and reviewing work.

ideas page

The Body and Keeping Healthy

Background

To keep healthy, you need to do a number of things: eat sensibly, take plenty of exercise and avoid health risks, such as germs, smoking, alcohol, drugs, etc.

Food is a mixture of useful substances: carbohydrate, fat, protein, fibre, minerals, vitamins and water. A balanced diet is one that gives you the right amounts of all these. Meat or meat alternatives such as nuts and pulses give energy and help build blood, muscle and skin. Dairy foods or calcium-enriched foods build strong teeth and bones. Fruit and vegetables keep hair, eyes and skin healthy. Bread, rice and potatoes can supply about half the body's energy. Sweets and sugary foods provide energy only and are of no other use. Any excess food is stored as fat under the skin.

The body needs about a litre of water a day. Much is lost through sweating and going to the toilet. Cells and blood in particular contain large amounts of water.

Germs are harmful microbes. Bacteria and viruses are microbes and cause diseases (NB. not all bacteria are harmful). Germs can be spread by droplets (sneezing and coughing), touching infected people, animals or objects, and dirty food and water. Personal cleanliness is essential to prevent germs spreading.

Activity pages

Your Body Has Many Parts

Learning objectives

- To identify external parts of the human body.
- To identify some internal body organs and bones.

Use nursery rhymes, poems and songs to introduce the idea of body parts. Discuss what the different parts of the body are for and how we keep them healthy and strong – diet, exercise, sleep.

Healthy Eating

Learning objectives

- To know that humans need a balanced diet to keep healthy.
- To know that too much sugary food can be bad for us.

Discuss the effects of not eating at all and then of not eating a balanced diet. Make a simple healthy snack, such as egg and cress sandwiches (wholemeal bread) followed by fruit salad. Compare this snack with crisps, cake, biscuits and fizzy drinks. What happens to the body if you eat only these 'treats'?

Keeping Clean

Learning objectives

- To be able to plan an investigation.
- To be able to make predictions.

Discuss why we wash our hands and what makes our hands dirty. Ask what times of the day the children wash their hands and what could happen if they did not wash them.

This investigation sets out to determine whether dirty hands are cleaned better by warm water or by cold water. The concept of fair testing is important; the only thing that is different is the temperature of the water. Control the variables by using the same amount of water, same size bowls, same vigour of scrubbing hands and length of time in the water, same quantity of soap (use a liquid dispenser), same amount of dirt on each set of hands. Provide a dirty substance, such as face paint to produce equally dirty hands.

Oral work

Discuss what other parts of our body we need to keep clean (e.g. hair, teeth, face), why we wash our bodies and what things help us to keep clean (e.g. soap, brush, flannel). Why is it important to keep clean and tidy (e.g. personal health and social reasons)?

Written work

The children could match the phrases 'Wash hands before' and 'Wash hands after' to various actions, such as using the toilet, getting food ready, eating food, touching pets, etc.

Carry out surveys and construct bar charts to illustrate data for: number of times hands are washed during the day, number of baths taken in one week, number of times teeth are cleaned during the day, favourite foods, etc.

The children could design posters to be displayed in the toilet areas warning others of the dangers of not washing hands.

ICT

Use an ICT package to present survey data as pictograms, pie charts or bar charts.

Your Body Has Many Parts

Key Idea Each part of the body has a different name and a special job.

- Label the body parts on the picture.
  Use the words below to help you.

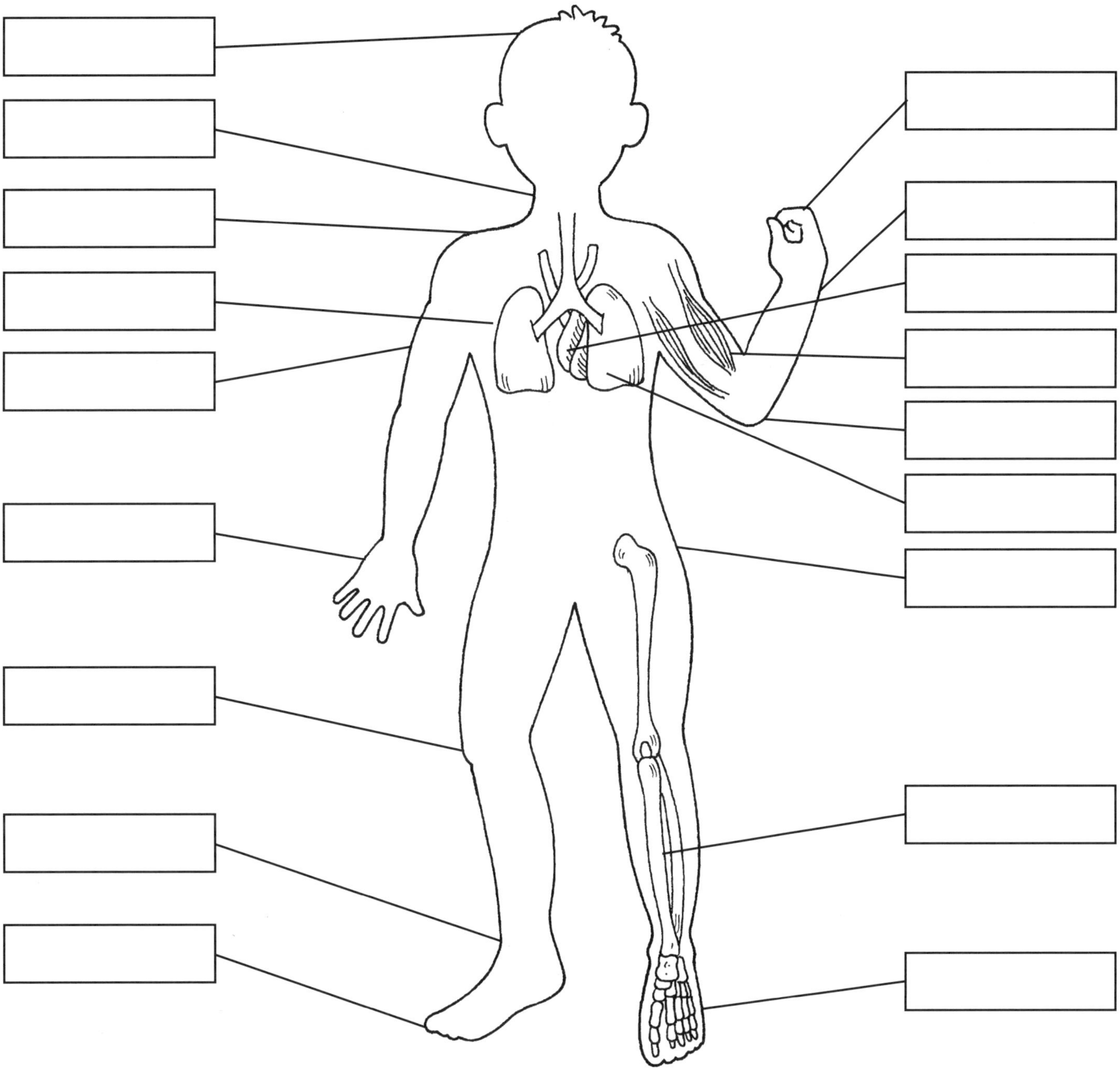

Head	Arm	Ankle	Hip	Wrist	Lung
Heart	Shoulder	Neck	Chest	Knee	Foot
Toes	Bones	Hand	Muscles	Elbow	Fingers

Healthy Eating

You will need

– Six different coloured crayons

Key Idea You need a balanced diet to stay healthy.

- Look at the table. Choose a different colour for each type of food and correctly colour the foods. Some foods may need to be two colours.

Type of food	Why our body needs it
Cereal	Foods to give us energy to do work and give us fibre.
Dairy foods	Foods to make us strong and help us to grow.
Fruit and vegetables	Foods to keep us healthy and help food move.
Meat, fish and meat alternatives	Foods to help us grow and repair any damage.
Fatty foods	Foods to give us energy to do work and keep us warm.
Sugary foods	Foods that only give us energy to do work.

Keeping Clean

You will need

- Bowl of warm water
- Bowl of cold water
- Soap
- Towels
- Dirty hands
- Clock

Key Idea You need to wash your hands to keep them free of dirt and germs.

- You are going to do an experiment to find out if warm water or cold water is better for cleaning dirty hands.

Title:

I think my hands will be easier to clean in the bowl of ______________________.

I think my hands will be more difficult to clean in the bowl of ______________________.

Here is a picture of my experiment:

I found out that:

Using ______________________

and ______________________

water made cleaning my hands easier.

It was more difficult to clean my hands using soap and ______________ water.

NOW Answer the following questions 'True' or 'False'.

a. Dirty hands might carry germs. [ ]

b. Dirty hands are easy to clean in cold water. [ ]

c. Soap helps to clean dirty hands. [ ]

d. Warm water helps to clean dirty hands better than cold water. [ ]

ideas page

Plants

Background

Plants can be divided into three main groups. Group 1: very simple plants without definite leaves, stem or roots. This includes bacteria, algae and fungi. Group 2: plants that make spores rather than seeds, such as moss and ferns. Group 3: plants that make seeds and have definite leaves, stem and roots. This group can be further divided into flowering plants that have seeds covered with a protective coat (fruit) and conifer plants, which produce uncovered seeds in cones.

Green plants can make their own food. They use carbon dioxide, water, a chemical called chlorophyll (which gives their green colour) and sunlight to make their food. Roots are needed to take in water and minerals and also to anchor the plant in the ground. The stem acts as an essential transport route carrying water and minerals. It also supports the leaves towards sunlight.

Activity pages

Parts of a Plant

Learning objectives

- To recognise simple characteristics of a plant.

Show the dandelion plant in the jar of water. Point out the veins in the leaves and note how they branch from a central main vein. These carry the water to the leaf and take away the food that is made in the leaf. Food is taken to parts of the plant that are growing.

Safety – The children should wash their hands after handling plants and soil.

Growing a Plant From Seed

Learning objectives

- To know that a seed contains a new plant.
- To know that a seed grows when given the correct conditions.

Flowering plants make seeds that grow into new plants. The seeds are dormant until the correct conditions of warmth, moisture (water) and air allow germination to occur. Seeds do not need soil to germinate. A seed contains a new plant and its food store. A tough skin covers it. Soaking the seed in water overnight will cause the seed to absorb water and the seed coat to split open. After about three days the root will appear followed by the shoot.

Wedge the pea seeds between the rolled paper and the jar. If necessary, to give extra support, material can be placed inside the rolled paper: use soil, sand, compost or paper.

Safety – The children should wash their hands after handling plants and soil.

Plants Where You Play

Learning objectives

- To be able to identify local plants in the immediate environment.
- To be able to observe and compare local plants.

The children should be given the activity sheet and asked to find the plants in the local area. They should be shown examples of each of the plants to include: roots, stem, leaves and flowers where possible. Discuss how each of the plants is different.

Safety – Ensure that the children are well supervised.

Oral work

Discuss the development of a plant: fruit with seed, to new small plant, to larger plant with young buds, to plant with flowers, to plant with fruits. You could use a pea, tomato or bean plant. Keep pods from a broad bean plant from the previous year to show how the fruit develops. Discuss different types of fruit: juicy ones that we eat, such as apples, pears, tomatoes; dry pods that pop open, such as beans, peas, wallflower, broom, geranium; light, feathery or winged ones that are carried by the wind, such as dandelion, sycamore, ash. A plant has fruit to feed the growing seeds and to help disperse the seeds.

Written work

Make a tree card that shows details of a particular tree. This could include a leaf print, a bark rubbing, an outline of the tree's shape, an outline of the tree's leaf shape, the tree trunk circumference.

Do observational drawings of plants (to include roots) and fruits.

ICT

Use a video showing time-lapse photography of a seed growing into a plant.

Parts of a Plant

You will need
- Scissors
- Glue

Key Idea A plant has different parts. Each part has a different job.

- Cut out the labels below and stick them on the sheet in the correct places.

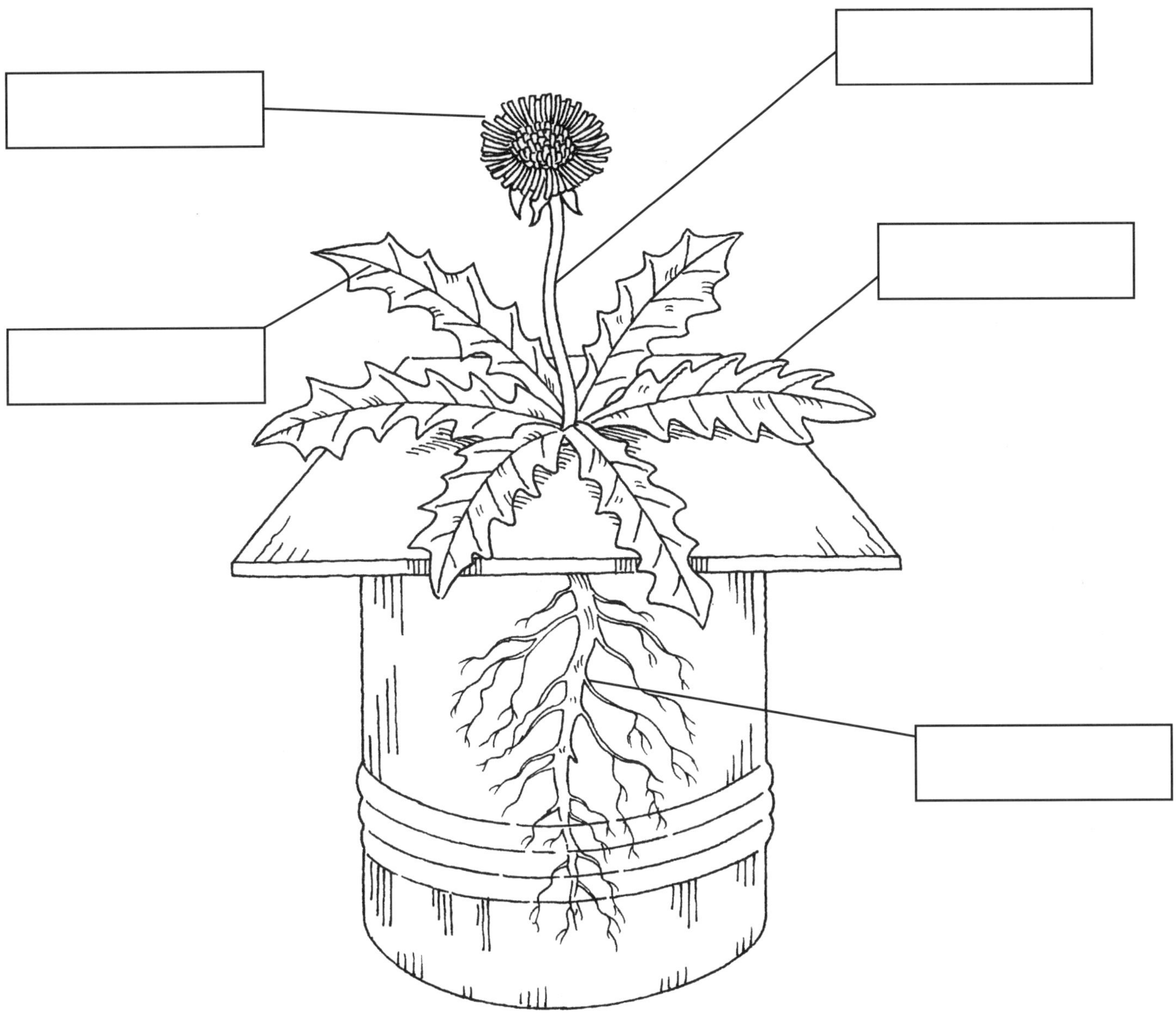

Flower

Leaf

Roots

Veins

Stem

Growing a Plant From Seed

You will need
- Pea seed
- Cut down plastic drink bottle
- Water
- Blotting paper

Key Idea Seeds grow into new plants. Seeds need warmth, water and air to grow into new plants.

1. Label the experiment below.

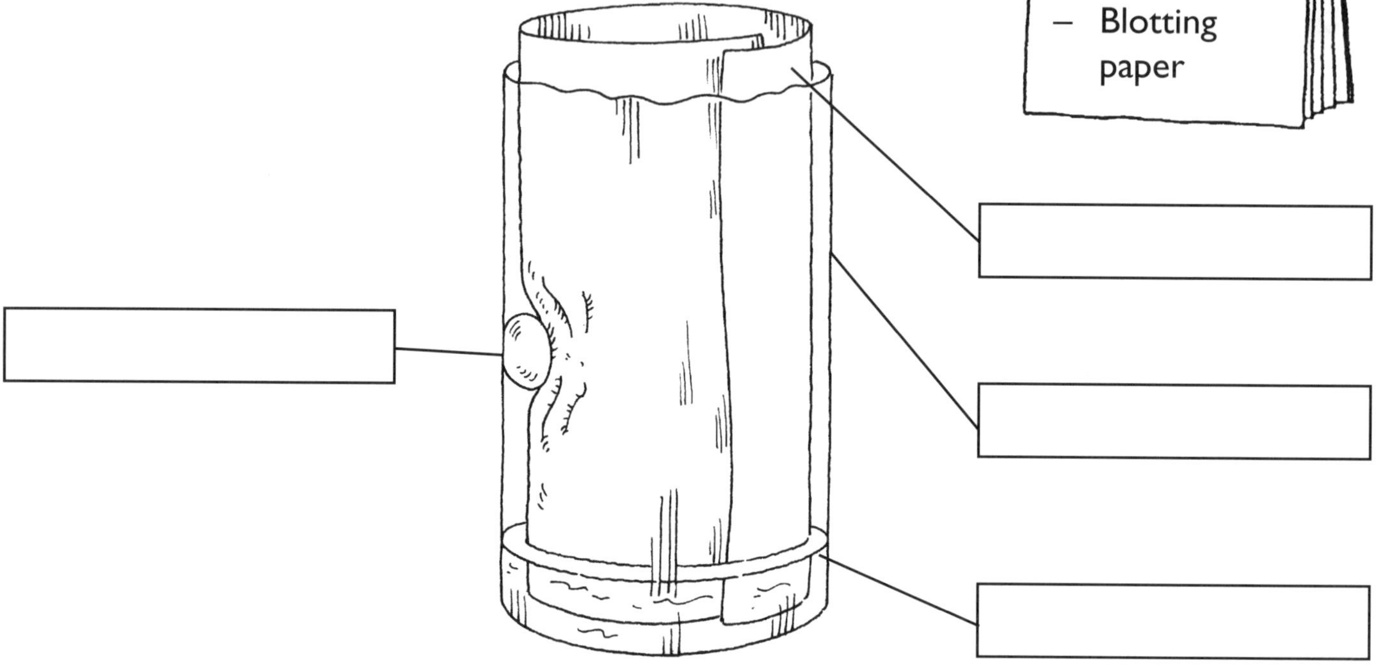

2. Look at the above picture and grow your own pea plant.

3. Look at your pea seed every day. On the chart below, fill in the number of the day when your pea seed looks like each of the pictures.

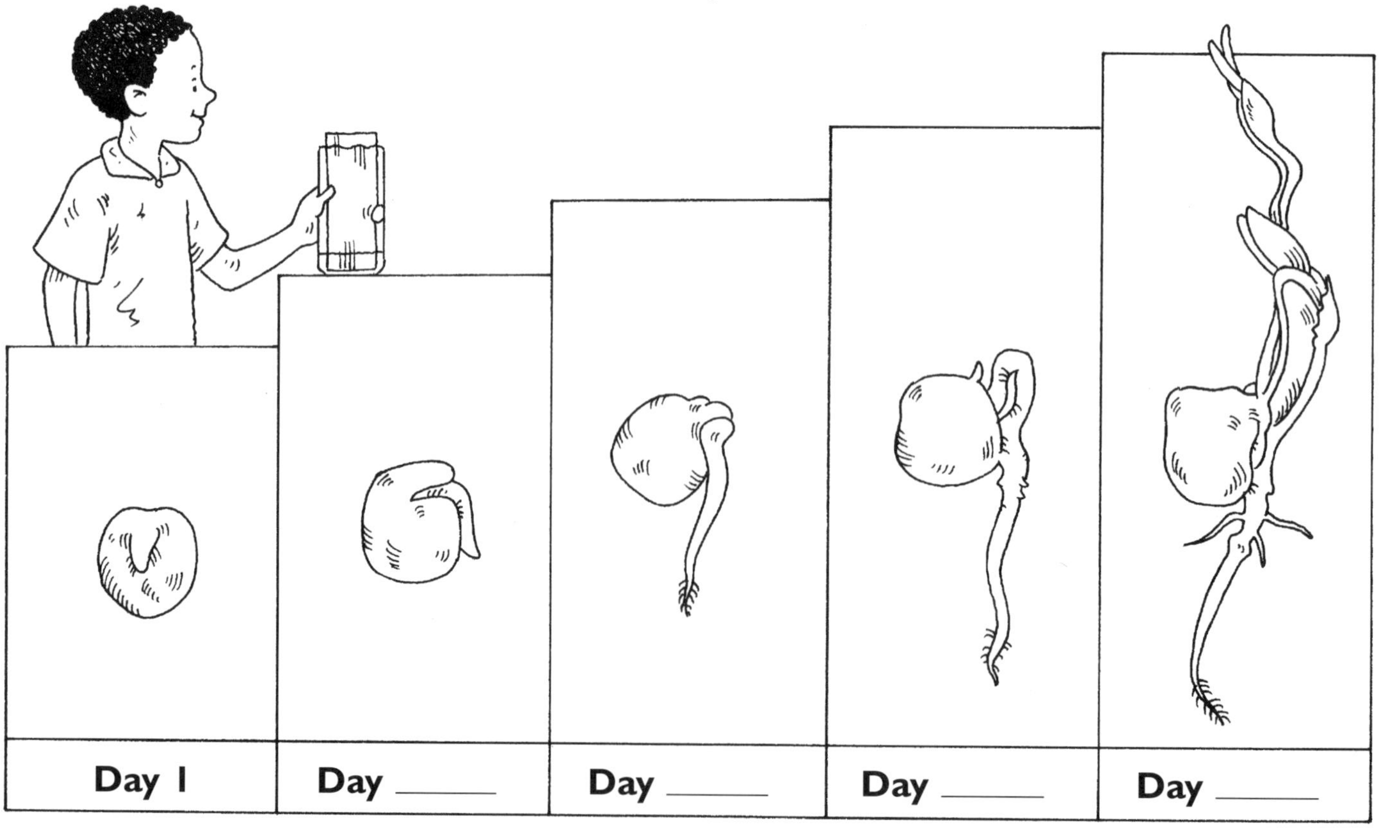

Plants Where You Play

Key Idea There are different types of plant all around us.

- In groups, look for each of the following plants in these places.

Open field	Near a hedge	On a path	Under a tree

Complete the table below. If you find the plant, put a tick.
If you cannot find the plant, put a cross.

Daisy

Dandelion

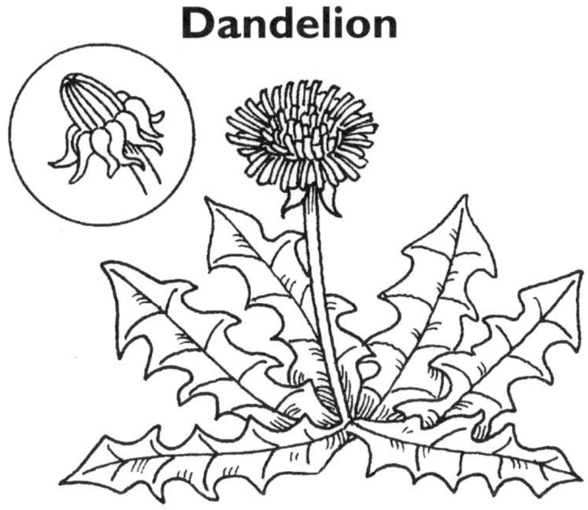

Buttercup

Plantain

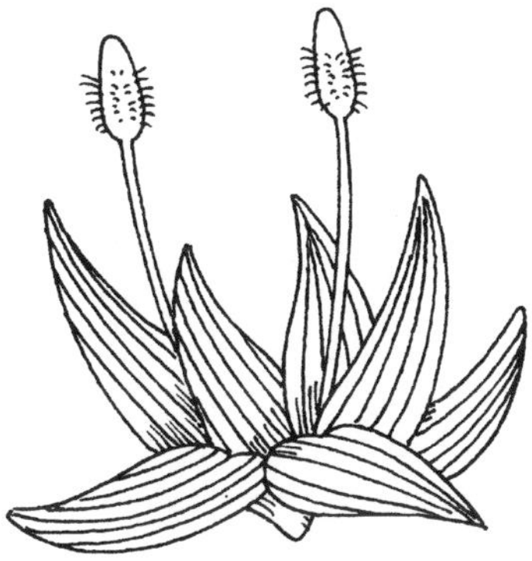

Clover

Moss

Plant	Location			
	Open field	Near a hedge	On a path	Under a tree
Daisy				
Dandelion				
Buttercup				
Plantain				
Clover				
Moss				

ideas page

Ourselves

Background

People throughout the world have the same body shape and share the same set of body organs, but no two people are alike. Even identical twins differ in some ways. Features such as weight, height, hair and eye colour, shape of face, language, personal likes and dislikes, habits and skills vary from person to person.

People occur in so many different sizes that it is possible to arrange a continuous line between two extremes, such as from tallest to smallest. Characteristics that have many intermediate types, such as height or weight, are said to show continuous variation. Discontinuous variation occurs where characteristics have few forms, such as being able to roll the tongue.

People inherit some characteristics from their parents (e.g. hair colour). These are determined before birth at the moment sex cells meet. Some characteristics, such as language, skills, scars are formed after birth and are called 'acquired characteristics'.

Activity pages

How We Differ

Learning objectives

- To identify ways in which humans are similar and different.
- To show sensitivity when discussing differences.
- To know that some features of appearance can easily be changed and others cannot.

Discuss visible differences between each other (e.g. hair, eyes, size, clothing) and then discuss how people are different in non-visible ways (skills, likes and dislikes). Point out that some features can be changed easily, such as hairstyle and clothes; but others cannot, such as height and body shape.

The children should sort the pictures on this activity sheet according to characteristics (e.g. young/old, short hair/long hair, glasses/no glasses). You could set the children the challenge of finding as many groups of opposite characteristics as possible.

Human Features

Learning objectives

- To know that humans are the same as each other in some ways, but different in others.
- To make observations and comparisons of human variation.

Use photographs of children and their families (or take them from a magazine) to stimulate discussion about similarities and differences between people. Characteristics are passed on from one generation to another through genes. Genes make up the code passed on from the mother and the father at conception. They will determine many human features. The chart looks at five features that depend largely on the genes in the body cells. They are inherited characteristics. The environment may affect some human characteristics, for example the Sun affects freckles. Freckles often fade in Winter because the Sun is not as strong.

Recording and Interpreting Data

Learning objectives

- To use comparative vocabulary in discussing differences in human characteristics.
- To be able to make simple interpretations from data shown in graphs, charts or tables.

Discuss the charts on this activity sheet to test the children's ability to interpret data. For example, for chart 1 you could ask, 'Who throws the beanbag 3m?', 'Who throws it the furthest?', 'Which two people's scores add up to 7m?'. Make comparisons between features, for example 'Do the tallest people have the longest shoe'.

Oral work

Discuss ways in which humans are alike: two eyes, two legs, etc.

Discuss how appearance changes over time: taller, heavier, older, etc.

Written work

Ask the children to draw head profiles or full-face views of each other and then guess who they are. Classify faces by shape, such as round, oval, square, oblong or heart shaped.

Design identity cards or booklets entitled 'All About Me'. Include a photo and details of characteristics, measurements of body parts, likes and dislikes, etc.

How We Differ

You will need

– Scissors

Key Idea

People are similar to each other in some ways and different in others.

1. Cut out the pictures below and sort them into two groups

2. Then sort them into two different groups.

Human Features

Key Idea There are a number of body features that depend on the genes that you have.

- Fill out the chart below with children from your class.

Child's name	 Can roll tongue  Cannot roll tongue	 Free ear lobe  Attached ear lobe	 Freckles  No freckles	 Right handed  Left handed	 Bent thumb  Straight thumb

Recording and Interpreting Data

Key Idea There are many ways of showing data, such as tables, bar charts and pictographs.

Distance beanbag thrown when sitting down

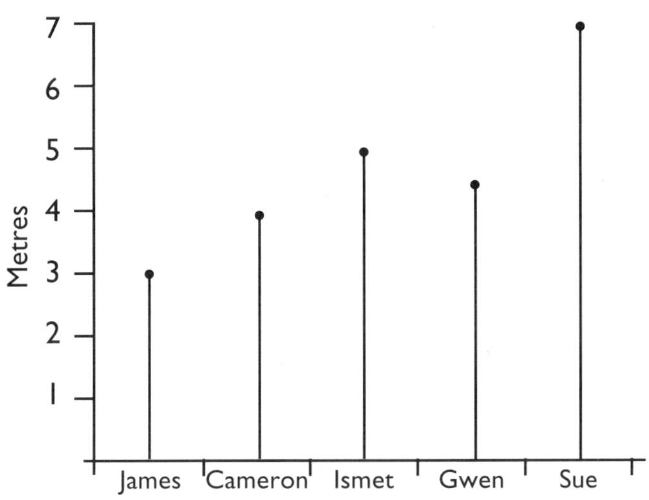

Eye colour in Class 2

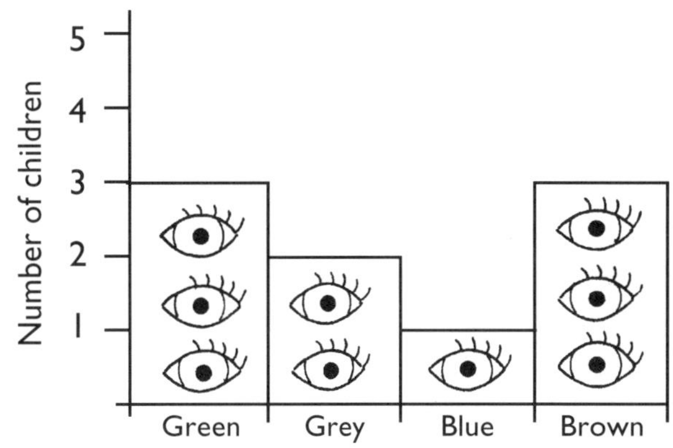

Joe has the smallest foot
Paul has the biggest foot

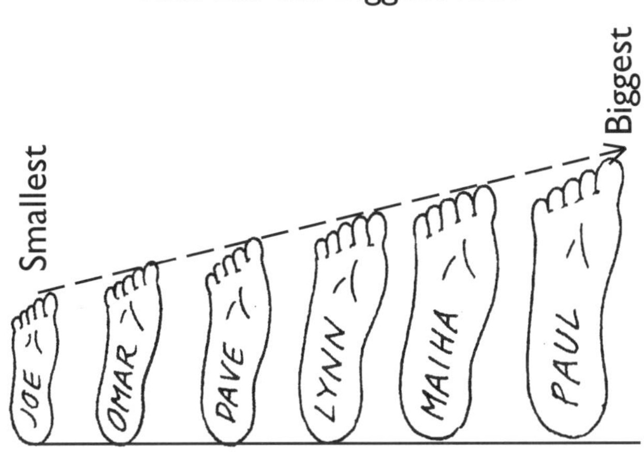

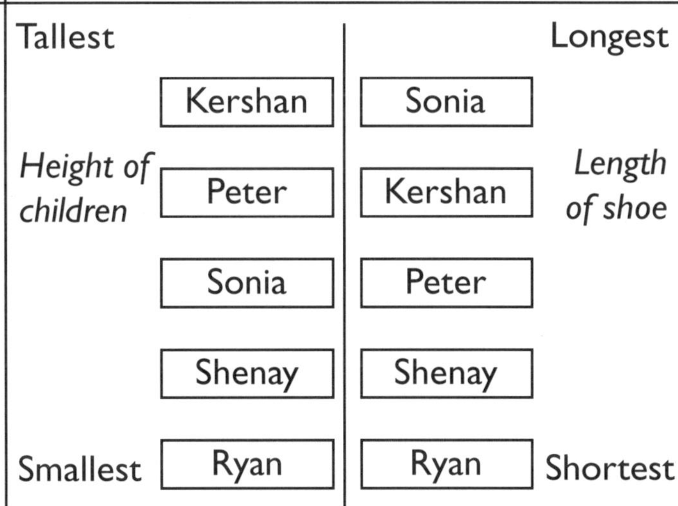

Do the people with the largest grab have the largest hand?

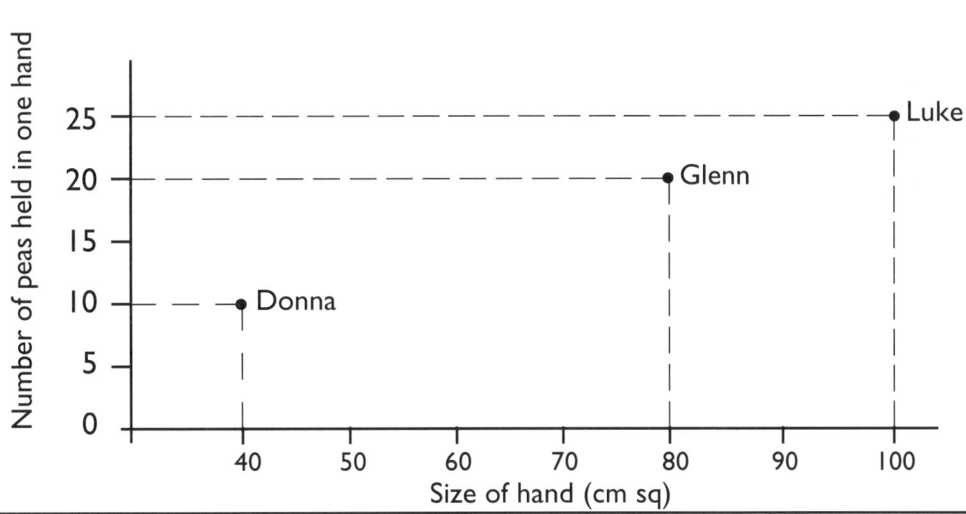

ideas page

Measuring Differences

Background

The Egyptians used their body parts to measure length. To overcome the problem that people were not all the same size, they used a standard unit of measurement called the cubit. They made a standard cubit rod to make measuring more accurate. The Romans measured the distance between towns using their foot steps.
1 Roman mile (mille passus) = 1000 paces
1 pace (passus) = 5 foot steps
1 foot (pes) = 12 unciae (thumb widths).

Even today the body is used to measure things. The height of a horse is measured in hands. The measurement of a fathom originates from lowering a rope into water. The rope was lowered and counted out using outstretched arms.

Activity pages

How Quick Are You?

Learning objectives

- To carry out fairly, an investigation on reactions.
- To present results as a block graph.

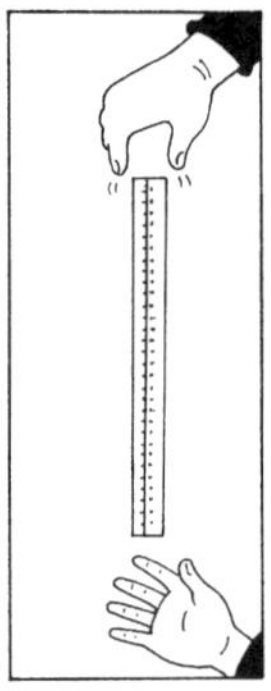

The children should work in pairs for this activity, with one child dropping the ruler and the other catching it. The ruler should always be held vertically with the number '0' at the bottom.

Determine what is a fair test, for example hold the ruler from the catching hand at an agreed distance (4cm); the ruler must not be thrown down; hold catching fingers open at about 6cm; do not allow the bottom finger to stop the ruler dropping through; measure from an agreed position (e.g. top of catching finger). If the child misses the ruler completely, call this 30cm. Show the children how to record their results as a block graph.

Do the Strongest Legs Have the Longest Jump?

Learning objectives

- To measure in standard units strength of legs and length of jump.
- To present measurements in a table and draw conclusions.

Readings can be obtained for both legs and the stronger leg recorded. Ensure that the children do not attempt to stand or hold the chair when pushing. Remind them that the jump is a standing jump. Allow three goes and record the best jump. Discuss what makes a no-jump and how to measure the length fairly.

Measuring Your Hand

Learning objectives

- To recognise that some differences can be measured.

Standard measurements can be used with the class. However, less able children will make simple visible comparisons of results, such as length of paper snip, length of string, number of seeds, how much the water level rises. More able children will measure the lengths of the paper snip and string in centimetres, weigh the seeds and measure the volume of water pushed out of the container. The centimetre squares can be counted to give standardised measurements or less able children can cut out the hands and place the templates over each other. Make comparisons, such as 'Does the biggest hand have the largest area?'.

Oral work

Discuss body comparisons, such as whether the child with the biggest feet has the biggest head or whether the child with the biggest feet is the tallest.

Whole-class activity

Measure group reaction time. Stand the whole class in a circle, holding hands. You should join the circle, while holding a stopwatch. Simultaneously, squeeze the hand of the child on your right and start the watch. This child squeezes the hand of the child on their right and so on. When the squeeze returns to you, stop the watch and record the time. Can the time be improved? You could try variations of this, such as a smaller circle, different times of the day, boys versus girls. You could also try measuring reaction time using a crocodile line with children passing on a tap on the shoulder. Stop the watch when the child at the end raises a hand.

ICT

Use CD-ROM to find out about early forms of measurement.

Use a data package to present results in a variety of ways, especially as block graphs.

How Quick Are You?

You will need

– 30cm ruler

Key Idea People have different skills and skills can often be improved through practice.

- You are going to do an experiment to find out how quickly you can catch a ruler and if you get quicker with practice.

Title:

What I think will happen is:

Here is a picture of my experiment:

My results table:

	Ruler caught at:		Ruler caught at:
Go 1		Go 6	
2		7	
3		8	
4		9	
5		10	

I found out that:

- Circle the correct sentences. To make my experiment fair:

a. I dropped the ruler downwards very hard. — I dropped the ruler carefully.

b. I always measured from the top of the finger. — I measured from anywhere on the ruler.

c. I only let my partner have one go at catching the ruler. — My partner had many goes.

Do the Strongest Legs Have the Longest Jump?

You will need
- Tape measure
- Bathroom scales
- Chair

Key Idea The strength of a part of the body can be compared with the job that part of the body does.

1. Measure, in centimetres, the distance you can jump from a line. Do this three times and record your best jump in the table.

Standing jump distance in centimetres	Strength of one leg in kilograms

2. Find out the strength of your leg. Sit on a chair and measure the force that one leg can push on bathroom scales. Measure the strength in kilograms. Now measure the force of the other leg. Write, in the table above, the measurement of the stronger leg.

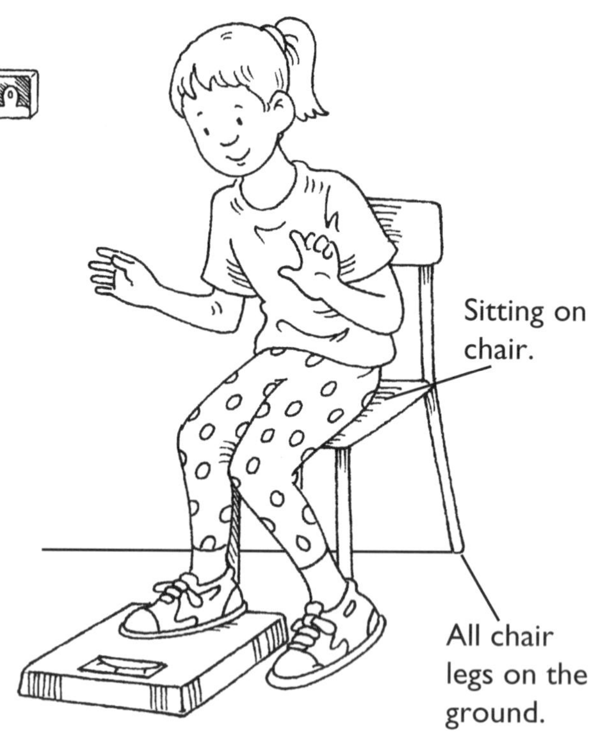

3. Draw out a table and write in the measurements for everyone in your class.

4. Who jumped the furthest?

5. Did the person who jumped the furthest have the strongest legs?

NOW Find out if the strongest arm has the furthest throw.

Measuring Your Hand

Key Idea

The size of your hands may be different from the size of your best friend's, Mum's, teacher's, brother's or sister's hands. The difference in size can be measured in many ways.

You will need

- Squared paper
- Plain paper
- Pencil
- String
- Scissors
- Strips of paper
- Container of seeds
- 1p coins
- Large jug of water
- Bowl
- Ruler
- Measuring cylinder

1. Measure your hand span using a strip of paper. Measure from the thumb to the small finger.

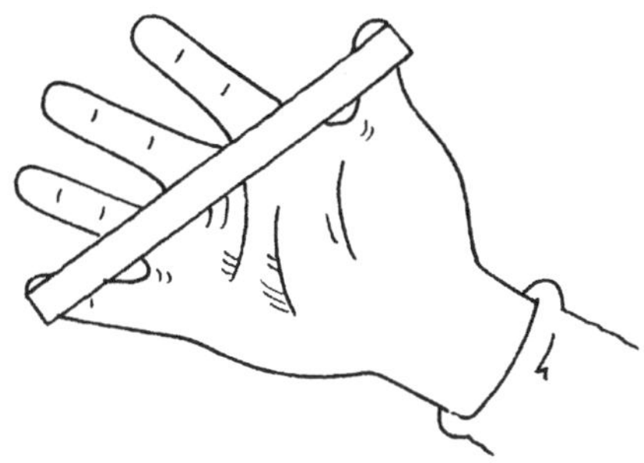

2. Draw around your hand on to squared paper. How many squares does your hand cover?

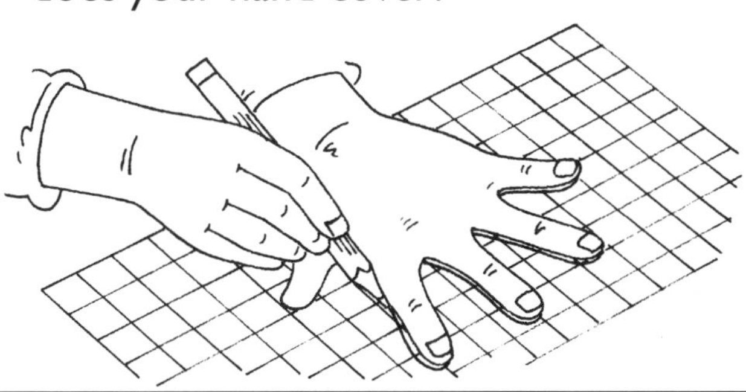

3. How many 1p coins are needed to cover the outline of your hand?

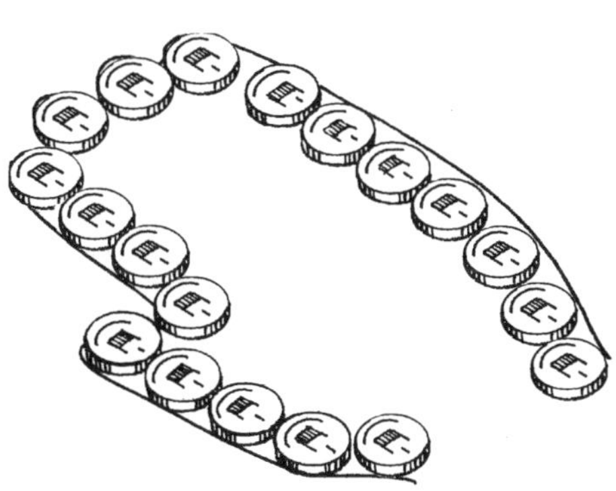

4. Place damp string around the outline. How long is the string?

5. How many seeds can you pick up with one grab?

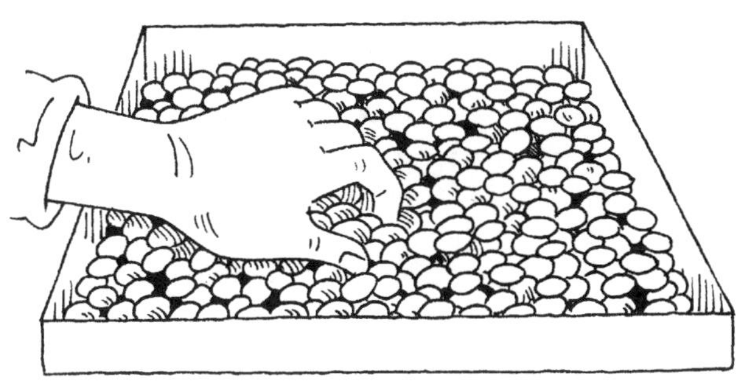

6. Lower your hand into a jug full of water. How much water is pushed out?

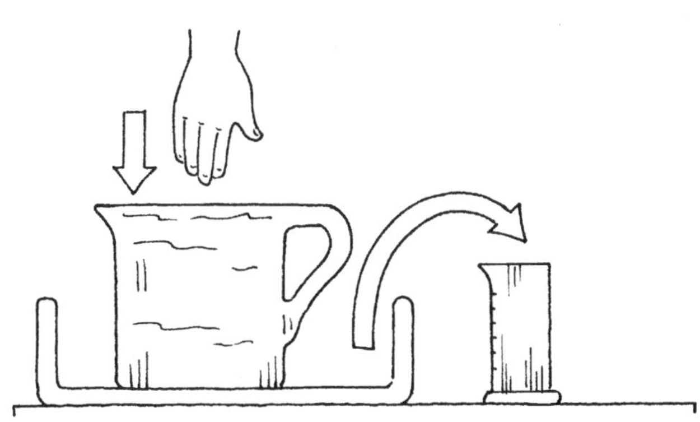

NOW Who has the biggest hands in your class? How do you know?

ideas page

Living Things

Background

Although all living things look different from each other, they share seven common characteristics. They all: 1. Feed, 2. Breathe (respire – use air to produce energy), 3. Grow, 4. Move, 5. Get rid of waste (excrete – remove unwanted chemicals that are made in the body such as carbon dioxide, water, urea, faeces), 6. Are sensitive (react to certain stimuli around them, e.g. green plants grow towards light; humans sweat in hot climates or shiver when cold), and 7. Reproduce.

Activity pages

Is it Alive?

Learning objectives

- To know what all living things have in common.
- To know that the group, 'living things', includes animals and plants.

The activity sheet shows examples of reacting (child holding nose, plant growing towards light), getting rid of waste (toilet, worm casts), feeding (fish eats fly, girl eats meal, dog eating), reproduction (chicken lays egg, cat with its kittens), growing (seed growing), breathing (diver), moving (hare). Some pictures could represent more than one characteristic.

Alive, Dead or Never Lived

Learning objectives

- To know whether something is alive, dead or has never lived.

Every living thing is made up from one or more cells. Most plants and animals are made up from millions of cells joined together. Dead things are still made up from cells, e.g. wood and leather used to be a living thing, so they are still made up of cells. Things that have never been alive are not made from cells.

Ask the class to sort the pictures into one of the three sets: 'Alive', 'Dead' or 'Never lived'. Glass, metal, and the teddy fit into the 'Never lived' group. Wool, chicken, fish fingers and wood fit into the 'Dead' group. First, identify those things that are living. From those remaining, identify which come from living things.

Animals Similar to Humans

Learning objectives

- To recognise similarities between humans and other animals.
- To recognise ways in which humans are different from other animals.

Discuss similarities between the animals in the pictures and humans (e.g. they have legs and arms, hair or fur, care for young, feed milk to babies, two eyes, two ears). Discuss differences (e.g. position of the eyes and ears, shape of nose, size of ears).

Oral work

Discuss the way living things move (whether they walk on two or four legs, slide, crawl, swim or fly). Discuss their covering (e.g. skin, fur, hair, scales, or feathers) and where they live (e.g. soil, trees, grass, stones, water, or cage).

Make a large collection of objects sorted into three categories – plants, animals and non-living. The latter can include natural and manufactured objects. Allow the children to handle and explore the characteristics of the objects on display. Discuss their similarities and differences.

In discussing the characteristics of living things, the idea of 'senses' could be introduced (e.g. humans react to certain smells, we react to different textures, certain sounds cause different responses).

Written work

Keep a daily diary of the activities you do in one day. This can then be used to discuss what living things do, such as eat, play (move), wash, sleep, watch TV (respond), etc.

ICT

Show a video of larger wild animals in their natural environments.

Is it Alive?

Key Idea Living things share a number of characteristics.

- Each picture shows one or more of the seven things that **all** living things do.

React	Get rid of waste	Feed	Have babies
Grow	Breathe	Move	

Choose one of the characteristics for each picture and write it in the box.

		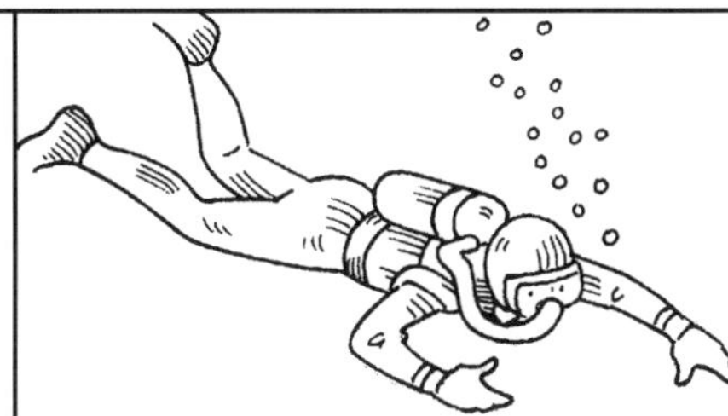
	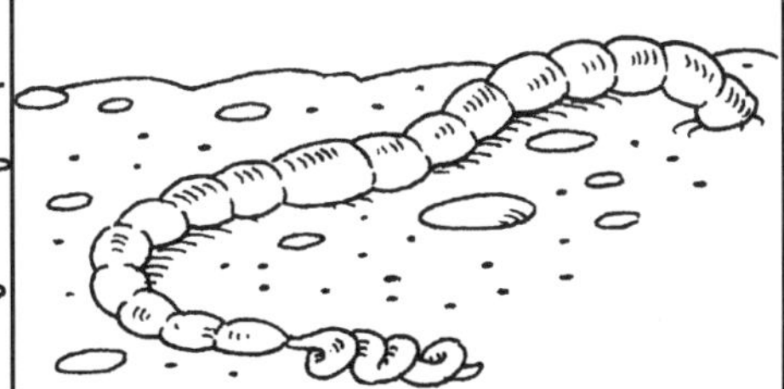	

NOW Look again at the pictures. Which ones could show more than one characteristic. Why?

Alive, Dead or Never Lived

You will need

– Scissors

Key Idea

Objects can be sorted into three groups – 'Alive', 'Dead' or 'Never lived'.

- Cut out each picture. Place each picture into one of three groups – 'Alive', 'Dead' or 'Never lived'.

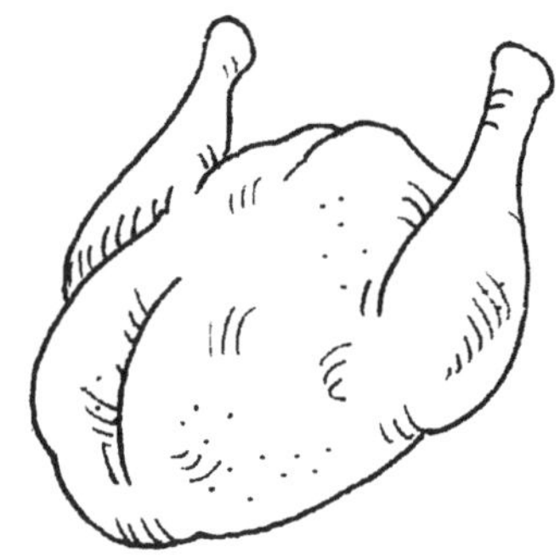

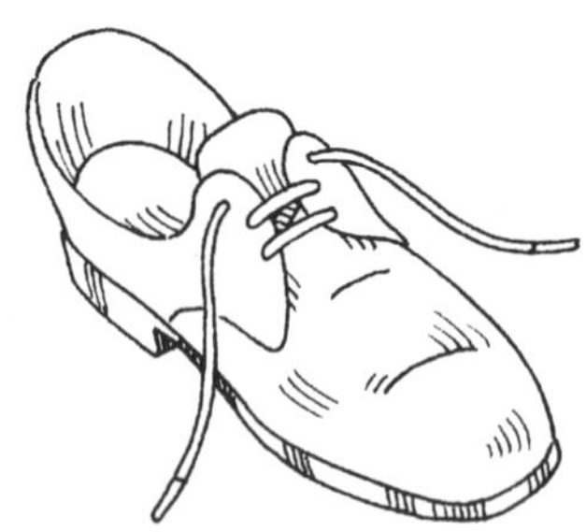

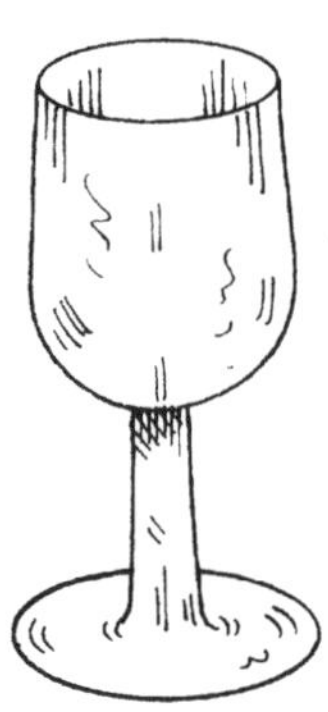

Animals Similar to Humans

Key Idea There are similarities between animals and humans. There are also some differences.

1. Look at these six different animal groups. How are they similar to each other?

2. Look at the heads and feet of these three animals.

a. In what ways are they similar?

b. In what ways are they different?

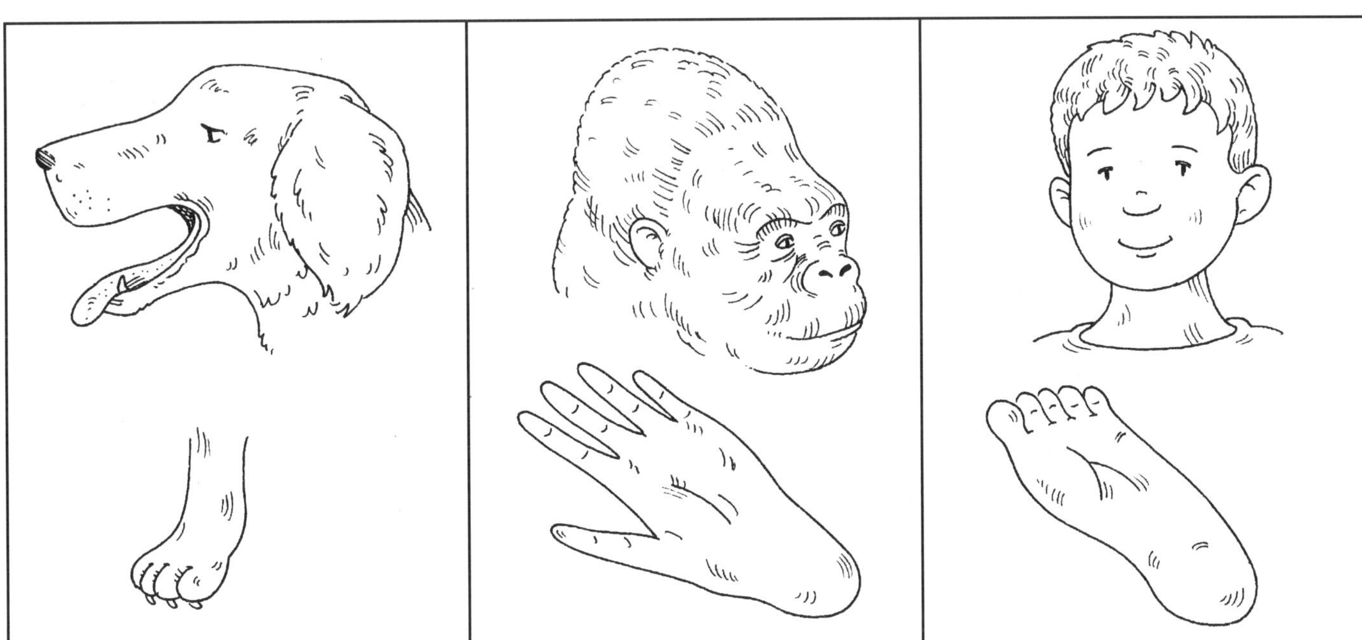

ideas page

Sorting Materials

Background

The characteristics of a material and how it behaves are called its **properties** (e.g. strong, flexible, transparent, waterproof, etc.). The eight main groups of materials are: wood, glass, rubber, metal, paper, plastic, fibre and stone. Some materials are found naturally and some materials are made in a factory (e.g. plastic, rubber, glass, paper and cloth). Some materials may be treated rather than manufactured (e.g. wood may be shaped and polished, metal heated and shaped).

Materials for display. (Hardware stores are very useful.)

1. **Wood:** fruit bowl, peg, ruler, sports bat, mallet
2. **Glass:** marbles, jam jar, bottle, light bulb
3. **Rubber:** rubber bands, wellington boot, kitchen gloves, cycle tyre
4. **Metals:** cutlery, large nail, can, tools, foil dish, scissors, nail file, coins
5. **Paper:** cardboard, newspaper, party plate, grease-proof
6. **Plastic:** comb, plate, cup, knives and forks, toys
7. **Fibres (cloth):** hats, gloves, scarf, slippers, teddy
8. **Natural materials:** feathers, shells, stones, pebbles, twigs, leaves, fruit, leather, bees' wax, fir cones, sheep's wool.

Activity pages

Using Your Senses

Learning objectives

- To use the senses to describe properties of objects.
- To recognise differences and similarities between objects.

Use a 'feely' bag with mystery objects inside. Ask the children to take turns to describe what they can feel. The children could describe how smooth, rough, flexible, hard, cold, etc. an object is.

Demonstrate the importance of smell. Ask the children to close their eyes. First, tell them that they are going to identify an object using only their ears. Take a jar half full of white vinegar and shake it vigorously. The group will guess that you are shaking a liquid. Show them the jar and ask them what they think the liquid is. Is it water? Remove the lid and ask for a volunteer to smell the liquid. Phew! It's white vinegar.

Ask children what parts of the body are important in identifying and describing objects. Are some senses more important than others?

Making Objects

Learning objectives

- To know how to sort materials into groups using appearance.
- To know that some materials are found naturally and some are treated and manufactured.

Ask the children to explore differences between naturally found objects and those treated or made in a factory. You could ask, 'What material is the ruler made from? What has been done at the factory to make the wood into a ruler?' Ask what is similar and what is different about a pair of objects. You could use stone vase and large pebble, wood log and wood chair, etc.

Using Materials

- To know that there is a wide range of materials with different properties.
- To know that materials have a variety of uses and are chosen to do specific jobs.
- To recognise and name common groups of materials.

Show the children an example of each of the eight material groups and ask questions, such as 'Why is the jar made of glass and not paper?', 'Why is the spanner made of metal and not rubber?'

Oral work

Ask a child to find an object that is, for example, flexible, made from a natural material, stretchy or squashy.

Give each child an object (see materials list). Call out a property (e.g. 'shiny'). The first child to call out 'snap' (if their material is shiny) wins.

Show the children four different objects. Prepare word labels that describe properties of materials and ask for volunteers to place a word label correctly on one of the objects.

Written work

Provide children with pictures of objects. Ask the children to label the picture or construct sentences to describe why certain materials have been used to make that object.

Using Your Senses

Key Idea You have five senses that send messages to your brain. Your brain tells the rest of your body what to do.

1. Complete the following sentences.

a. I see with my ______________ .

b. I ______________ with my ears.

c. I ______________ with my nose.

d. I ______________ with my tongue.

e. I feel with my ______________ .

Eyes – see

Ears – hear

Nose – smell

Tongue – taste

Skin – feel

2. Label the picture with the brain and the senses.

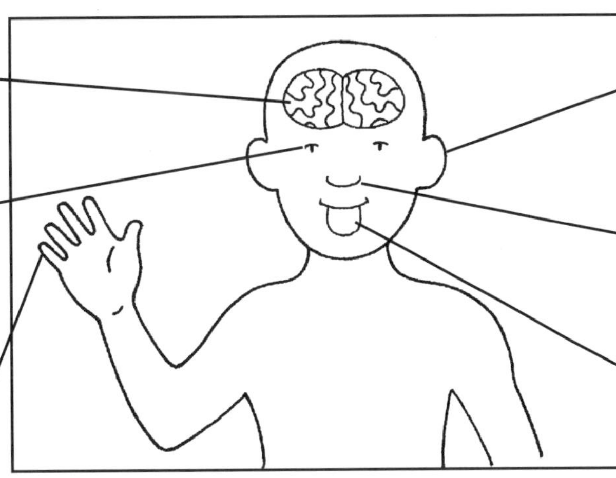

3. Tick which senses you use to experience each of the objects in the table.
You may use more than one.

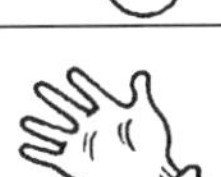								

Making Objects

Key Idea Natural objects are often changed in some way so that they can be used in everyday life.

1. Look at the pictures. Draw the order in which the four natural materials are changed to make the final objects.

 Sheep	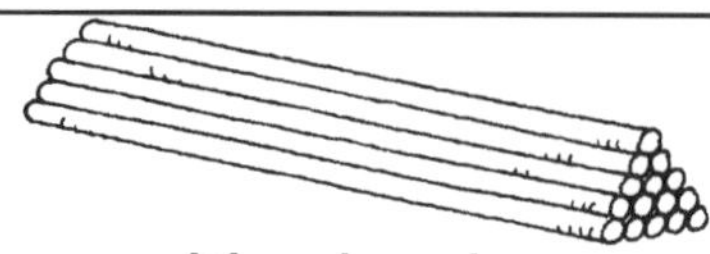 Metal rods	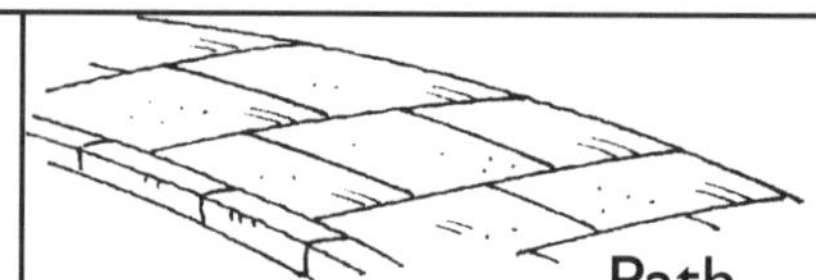 Path
 Stone	 Ball of wool	 Shoes
 Cow	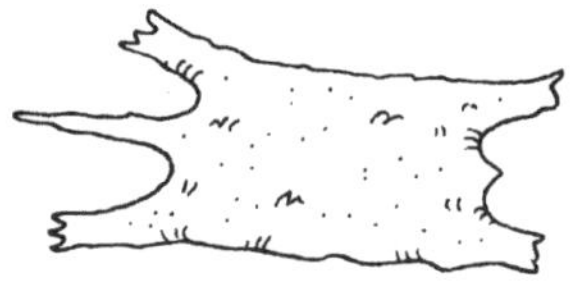 Animal skin	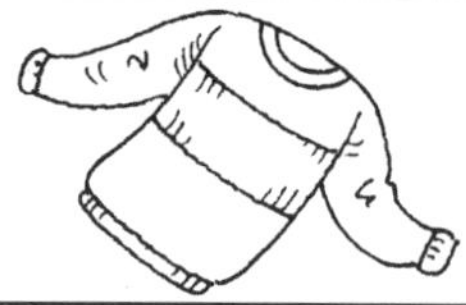 Jumper
 Metal ore	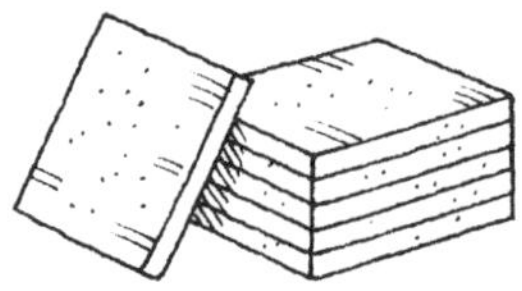 Paving slabs	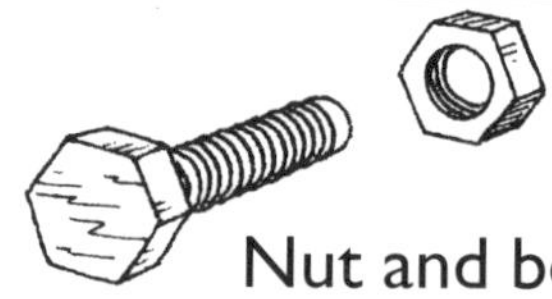 Nut and bolt

NOW Choose one of the natural materials and describe what has to happen to change it to make the final object.

Using Materials

Key Idea Materials have certain properties that are needed when making everyday objects.

1. Label the materials used in the objects below. Use the words to help. The first one has been done for you.

Brick	Wood	Metal	Glass	Plastic	Rubber

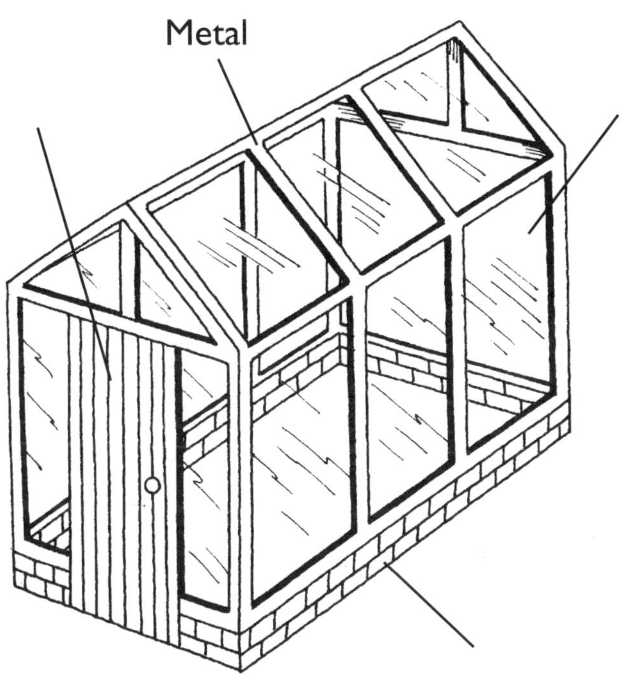

2. Draw lines to match each material to what it is like in the pictures above. The first one has been done for you.

a.	Brick	Heavy / Stretchy
b.	Wood	Weak / Not flexible
c.	Metal	Soft / Strong
d.	Glass	Spongy / Transparent
e.	Plastic	Hard / Warm
f.	Rubber	Squashy / Shiny

ideas page

Changing Materials

Background

Some materials can be changed into something that has different properties (e.g. water can be turned into ice) and sometimes the materials are changed permanently (e.g. heating clay, rotting food stuffs.)

Clay is a natural material and changes when dried or baked. Clay when mixed with water becomes soft. When dried in air, the water between the clay particles evaporates and the clay becomes hard. Adding water returns it to its soft state. If clay is handled for some time it becomes less malleable and may crack because heat from the hands dries it out. Clay that is dried in air is brittle. Baked clay is stronger. When clay is baked in a kiln the clay particles join together permanently. Adding water again will not return the clay to its soft state.

Activity pages

Melting Ice

Learning objectives

- To know that ice is frozen water and melts when warmed.
- To be able to design a fair test.

The activity investigates ice melting on dishes of different colours. Use paint (oiled-based or spray) to colour metal or paper dishes: you need to compare black and white. Other colours can be used to make a larger comparison.

Discuss the importance of keeping things the same but changing only the colour of the dish. Variables are dish colour, dish size, material of dish, size of ice cube, position of dish, time experiment started and stopped. Discuss with the children how they are going to record their results, how long they will leave the ice and how will they know which ice cube has melted the most.

Safety – Children should be aware of the dangers of handling ice. It can cause skin burns if handled immediately from the freezer.

Changing Clay

Learning objectives

- To know that some materials can be changed when heated.
- To know that some materials can be squashed, stretched, etc.

Discuss the properties of wet clay (e.g. soft, squashy, stretchy, can be rolled). Compare wet clay, clay dried in air and clay dried in an oven by looking at the following properties: texture, waterproofing, strength. Show some baked glazed and unglazed clay pots.

Decaying Materials

Learning objectives

- To know that some materials decay and some do not.

Discuss what happens to our weekly rubbish once it has been collected (e.g. burnt, recycled, squashed, landfill) and compare this with what would have happened to rubbish of the past (i.e. a tip at the bottom of the garden or outside the town). This leads us on to the concept that some materials decay and some do not (i.e. Roman coins and weapons are found regularly but clothing and food are much rarer).

In the activity, an example of each of the eight materials is placed into a jar of wet garden soil. Leave each jar for at least six weeks, although the contents could be viewed every two weeks.

Oral work

Allow children to explore ice blocks. Discuss how you could make ice melt more quickly and how you could stop it melting.

Discuss how materials can be prevented from decaying (e.g. wood – use paint, creosote; metal – paint, grease; food – air-tight containers, cans freezers, keep cool; cloth – keep dry).

Written work

Write a set of instructions to make a clay pot.

Design word bubbles where the shape of the bubble reflects the meaning of the word, for example:

ICT

Use CD-ROM to find out how clay bricks are made.

Melting Ice

You will need

- Sunny day
- Ice cubes
- Coloured dishes
- Clock

Key Idea

Ice is frozen water. Ice melts when it is warmed.

- You are going to do an experiment to find out if ice melts at different speeds when placed on different coloured dishes.

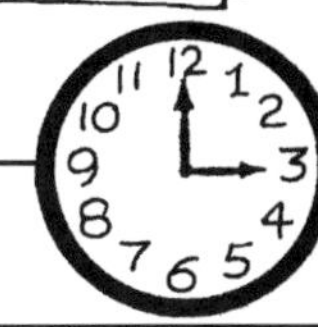

Title:

What I think will happen is:

Here is a picture of my experiment:

This is what did happen in my experiment:

I found out that:

1. The ice cube melted quicker on the ______________ coloured dish.

2. The ______________ coloured dish kept the ice the coolest.

3. To keep cool on a hot day, I would wear ______________ coloured clothes.

Changing Clay

You will need

– Scissors
– Glue

Key Idea Clay from the earth can be changed to make a waterproof pot.

- Cut out the sentences at the bottom of the page. Stick each on to the correct picture. Number the pictures in the correct order.

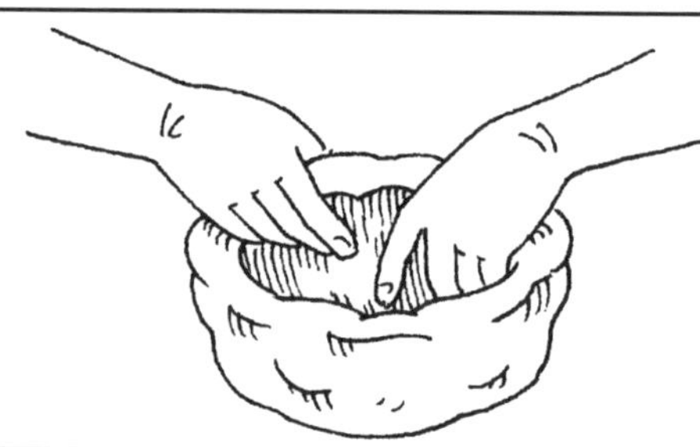

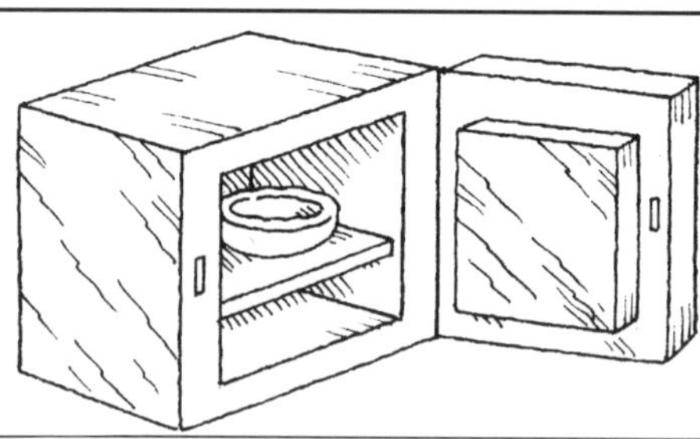

Add water to the clay and knead it to make it soft.	Dig up the clay.
Cover the pot with glaze.	Bake the pot in the oven. This makes it hard and strong.
Shape the clay into a pot by squashing and pushing it.	Bake the glazed pot. This makes it waterproof.

Decaying Materials

You will need
- Eight jars of wet soil
- Objects as below

Key Idea Some materials decay and some do not.

1. What do you think will happen to each of the materials when they have been left in wet soil for some time? Write the words in the space around the objects.

Rotten	Torn	Broken	Rusty	Shrivelled
Crumbly	No change	Smelly	Hard	Soft

Paper towel	Plastic spoon	Glass jar	Metal nail
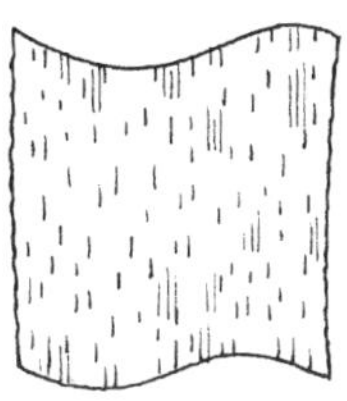		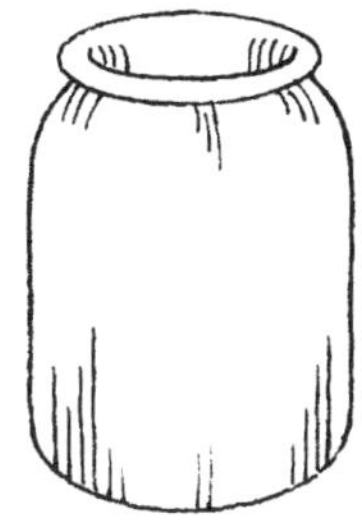	
Rubber band	Cotton cloth	Wooden peg	Apple core
	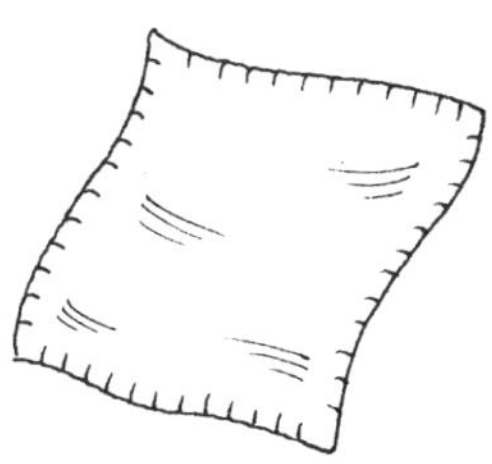		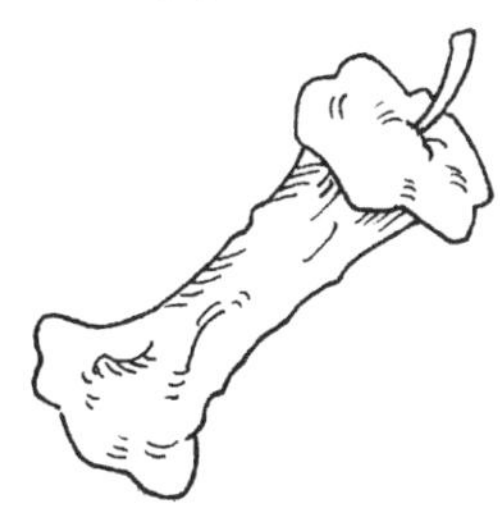

2. Now, what did happen to each of the materials? Use the words to fill in the table.

Material	**Description of material**
Paper towel	
Plastic spoon	
Glass jar	
Metal nail	
Rubber band	
Cotton cloth	
Wooden peg	
Apple core	

ideas page

Pushes and Pulls

Background

To make an object move you need a force. Pulls and pushes are both types of forces and they can alter an object in one or more ways. A force can change an object's speed by starting it moving or making it go faster or slower, by stopping it moving completely, by changing the direction in which the object is moving or by changing the object's shape. Whenever something moves or stops moving, slows down or speeds up, changes shape or direction, then a push or pull action has taken place.

Many words can describe a push or pull action: twist, twirl, squeeze, squash, stretch, bend, tear, drag, slide and hit.

Activity pages

Pushing and Pulling Objects

Learning objectives

- To know that pushes and pulls make things move.
- To know that pushes and pulls are forces.
- To know that there are many words that can describe a push or pull action.

Introduce the lesson by placing a brick on a cloth over a board and asking the children how they could move the brick without touching it with their hands (e.g. use other body part, poke it with an object, lift board, drag the cloth). Discuss words that describe the push or pull actions. For example, 'slide', 'drag'.

The Push of Air

Learning objectives

- To know that air can push and make things move.
- To know that a bigger push will speed things up.

Introduce the lesson by inflating a balloon and asking the children what will happen to the balloon if you let go. Add a short straw to the neck of the balloon by taping it securely. Show that the moving air can be used to make things move (e.g. scraps of paper, paper windmill). Show a ready-made balloon buggy model and ask questions, such as 'Which direction will it move?', ' What is the best surface to test it out on?', 'How can we make it go further?', 'Why does it eventually stop?'.

Pulling a Rubber Band

Learning objectives

- To be able to decide whether a test is fair.
- To be able to show results as a block graph.
- To know that a pulling force changes the shape of a rubber band.

Introduce the lesson by stretching a rubber band in your hands. Ask, 'What makes the band longer?'. Ask the children to describe what has happened to the band (e.g. stretched, changed shape). Compare pulling forces on different sized bands. Stretch the band by attaching a cup to it as in the experiment. (You could use paper-coated plastic cups from fast-food outlets.) Demonstrate what happens when marbles are added to the cup. Show the basic idea of the experiment and discuss the idea of making it a fair test (e.g. use marbles of the same size, place marbles into cup carefully and not by throwing).

Use a rubber band about 65mm long and 1mm thick.

Oral work

Build up a word bank for class display. This should show push and pull action words (e.g. 'squash', 'squeeze', 'bang', 'hit', 'twist', 'loosen', etc.). Discuss and demonstrate these different types of actions.

During the 'The Push of Air' activity, encourage a language of direction and speed (e.g. 'backwards', 'forwards', 'faster', 'slower', 'start', 'stop'). Introduce the idea of friction.

Written work

Find out how windmills work.

Find out about the destructive force of tornadoes and hurricanes.

ICT

Use a video such as the BBC's *Cat's Eyes* series on forces.

Pushing and Pulling Objects

You will need

– Magazines

Key Idea Pushes and pulls are forces that make things move.

- Which action pictures are pulls and which are pushes? Some may be pushes and pulls. Write your answers in the boxes. The first one has been done for you.

Pull		

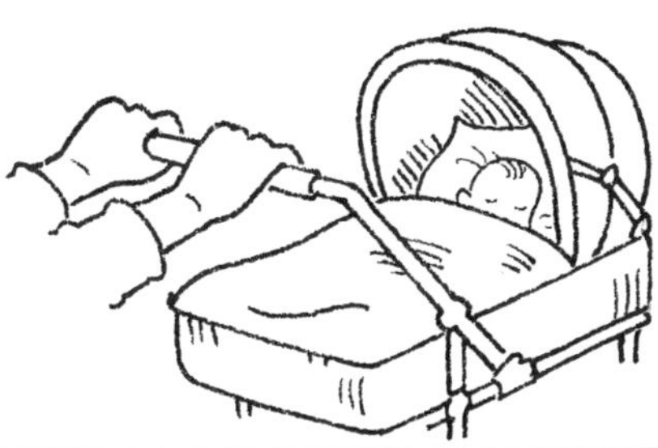		

NOW Collect some pictures from magazines that show a push or pull action. Write which are pulls and which are pushes.

The Push of Air

Key Idea Moving air can make things move.

You will need
- Card
- Three straws
- Barbecue sticks
- Four bottle tops (plastic milk carton)
- Tape
- Scissors
- Balloon

- Make your own balloon buggy.

Top view of base

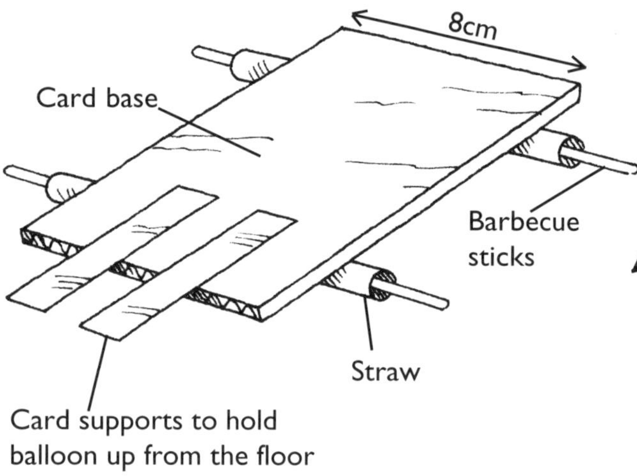

Bottom view of base

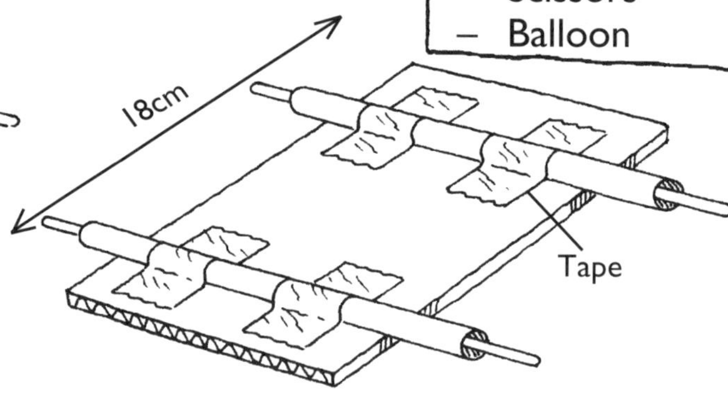

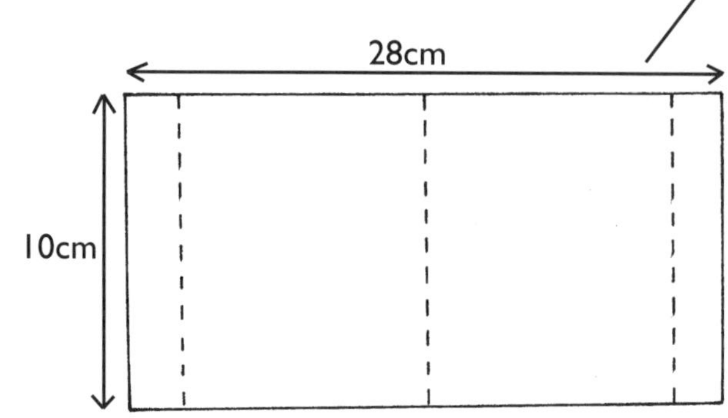

Fold card

Pulling a Rubber Band

Key Idea A rubber band can be made longer by a pulling force. When the force is taken away the rubber band pulls back to its starting length.

You will need

- Two desks
- Wood support
- Rubber band
- Plastic cup
- String
- Paper
- Tape
- Scissors
- Wire hook
- 50 marbles
- Glue

1. Set up your experiment.

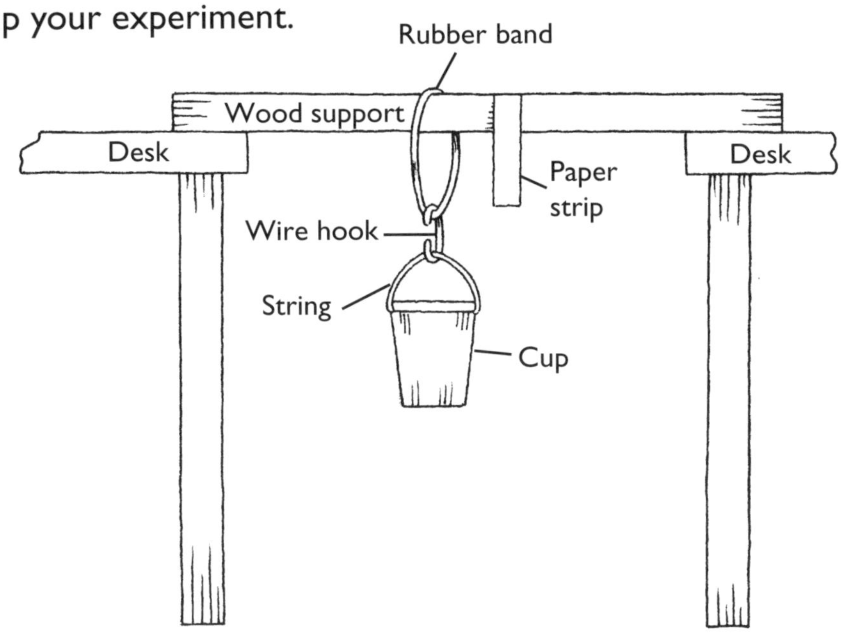

2. Hang the cup from the band. Cut a strip of paper the same length as the rubber band. Write '0 marbles' on your strip of paper.

3. Add 10 marbles to your cup. Cut a strip of paper showing the new length of the band. Write '10 marbles' on your strip of paper.

4. Add 10 more marbles to your cup. Cut a strip of paper showing the new length of the band. Write '20 marbles' on your strip of paper.

5. Now add 10 more marbles to your cup. Cut a strip of paper showing the new length of the band. Write '30 marbles' on your strip of paper.

6. Do this again and again until you have 50 marbles in your cup and six strips of paper.

NOW

Stick your paper strips side by side on a piece of paper.
Use your results chart to answer these questions.

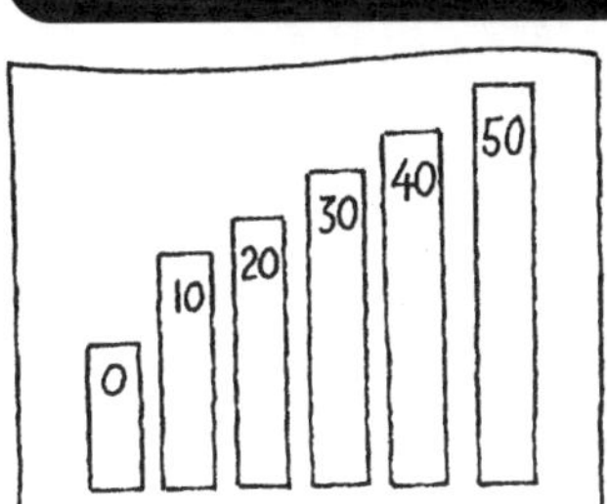

a. Estimate how long the paper strip would be if you had 60 marbles in the cup.

b. Estimate how long the rubber band would be if you had 25 marbles in the cup.

ideas page

Investigating Forces

Background

These activities offer the children the opportunity to carry out whole investigations. The teacher manages and sets the problems and allows the children to make guesses and predict what will happen in their experiments. They are able to plan and carry out practical tests that they have designed to be fair. The children have the opportunity to measure and record results, and evaluate and draw conclusions from them. They will have to decide whether these results support or refute their original hypothesis.

Variables that alter the way the can rolls are: the length of the slope, start position on the ramp, weight of can (empty or full), size of can, force at which can is released on the slope, slope height, surface on which the can rolls (rough or smooth), etc.

Activity pages

Which Can Rolls the Furthest?

Learning objectives

- To be able to decide whether an investigation is fair.
- To be able to make measurements in standard units.
- To be able to record measurements in a table.

The activity investigates rolling cans down a slope and measuring the rolled distance. It compares cans of the same size but different weights. Take two identical cans. Keep one can intact and remove both ends and the contents of the other can.

Introduce the activity by discussing rolling cans or toys on a flat surface. The children should realise that how hard you push the can and the surface on which it rolls will make a difference to how far the can travels. Slopes can be made as on page 38 using books and stiff card, plastic or wood. Establish the idea of fair testing and being able to make a fair comparison between the two cans.

Planning a Fair Experiment

Learning objectives

- To be able to decide whether an investigation is fair.
- To be able to explain how a comparison is made a fair test.
- To be able to recognise several factors that can be investigated.

This activity requires the children to discuss an imaginary experiment that investigates which car travels further when rolled down a ramp. Discuss with the children why the experiment is not a fair comparison.

Introduce the activity by rolling toy cars down a ramp. Discuss what makes a difference to how far the car travels along the floor from the ramp. Lead the children into making suggestions.

High Slope or Low Slope

Learning objectives

- To be able to make a prediction as to what will happen.
- To be able to plan and design a fair comparison.

This activity requires the children to design their own investigation to determine how the height of the slope alters the distance that an empty can rolls. The children will need to think about controlling variables empty to make a fair test. They will also need to recognise that measuring from a set starting point to an agreed finishing point is important (e.g. bottom of ramp to the back of the can).

Oral work

The discussion work should allow the children to understand the need to make the test fair; comparisons are made when variables are controlled. If the cans hit an object or veer to the side, reinforce the idea of repeated goes.

Written work

Compare cans with different skins (e.g. cans wrapped in fur, sandpaper, newspaper or rubber bands).

Compare cans let go at different positions on the slope.

Compare cans on slopes set at different heights.

Compare cans rolling off a slope on to different surfaces (e.g. carpet, wood, tiles or concrete).

Compare wind-up toys. Find out how far a clockwork toy will travel if you turn the key two times, then four times, then six times, etc. How would you make this a fair comparison (e.g. you could time how long the toy keeps moving)?

ICT

Use a video such as the BBC's *Cat's Eyes* series on forces.

Which Can Rolls the Furthest?

Key Idea

Weight can affect the rolled distance of an object.

You will need

- Empty can
- Full can
- Books
- Stiff card, plastic or wood
- Tape measure

- You are going to do an experiment to find out whether an empty can or a full can travels further along the floor when rolled down a slope.

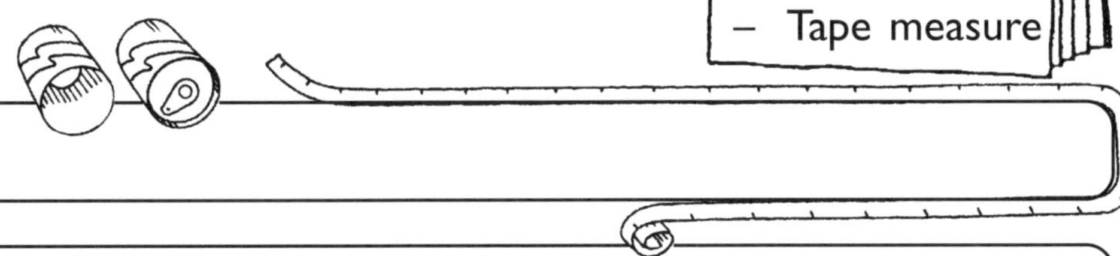

Title:

What I think will happen is:

Here is a picture of my experiment:

My results table:

	Distance rolled (cm)	
	Empty can	**Full can**
First go		
Second go		
Third go		
Fourth go		

I found out that:

Planning a Fair Experiment

Key Idea A test must be fair.

Jane wanted to find out which car travelled further along the floor when rolled down a slope. Here is her experiment. Find four reasons why Jane's experiment is not a fair one.

Jane's title: A car race

Here is a picture of Jane's experiment:

Car 1

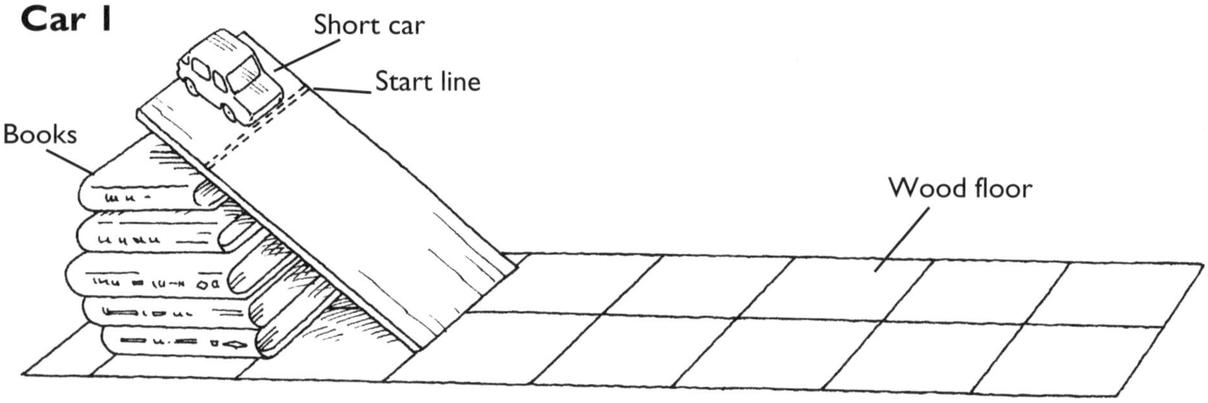

Car 2

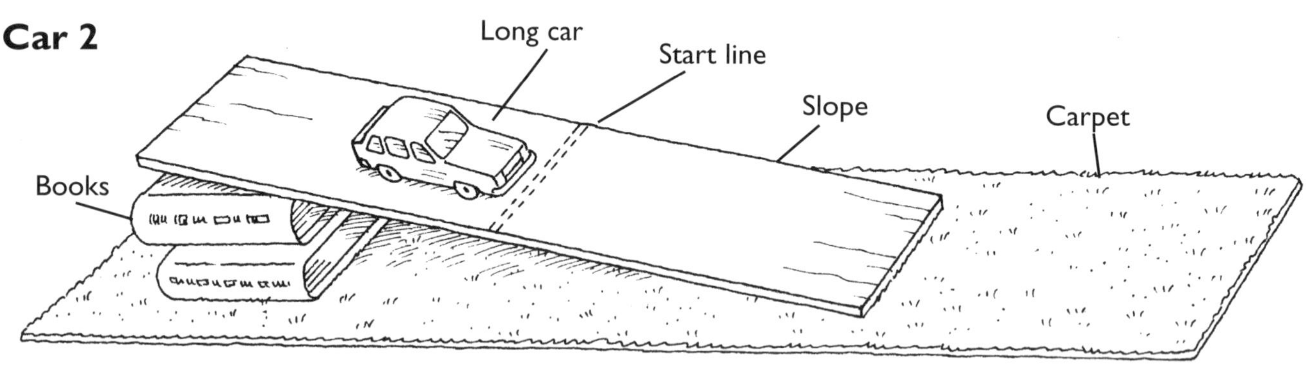

Jane's results table:

	Distance travelled (cm)	
	Car 1	**Car 2**
First go	56cm	19cm
Second go	53cm	26cm

Jane found out that:

Car 1 was better than car 2 because it travelled further.

High Slope or Low Slope?

You will need
- Empty can
- Books
- Stiff card, plastic or wood
- Tape measure

Key Idea The height of a slope can affect the rolled distance of an object.

You are going to do an experiment to find out how the height of a slope affects the distance that an empty can rolls.

Title:

What I think will happen is:

Here is a picture of my experiment:

My results table:

	Distance can rolled (cm)
2 books	
4 books	
6 books	
8 books	

I found out that:

because:

ideas page

Simple Circuits

Background

The scientific name for a single battery is a cell. Teachers will have to decide whether it is appropriate to make this distinction at this level. Cell holders can house size AA or C cells. The latter are larger and easier to handle. Some suppliers can offer AA holders with wires built in and therefore avoid the need for the battery snap tops to be used. Putting batteries into the holders can be awkward. The flat end of the cell must be placed on to the spring.

Match cells to + and – signs inside the holder.

Bulb holders will be a standard size for MES bulbs but they are available in batten, economy or clip-on type. Use 2.5V bulbs if two new 1.5V cells are used. 1.5V bulbs can be used if the cells are slightly worn or if only one 1.5V cell is used.

Activity pages

Circuit Problems
Learning objectives
- To know that a complete circuit is needed to make the bulb light.
- To be able to identify whether a simple circuit will work or not.

Part two of the activity requires the children to light up the bulb with the use of a holder. Putting the cells into the holders can be difficult for some children. Cut one wire of the cell holder so that the two wires are different lengths. This will stop accidental touching of the two wires and prevent a short circuit. In such a case the cells may get very hot and lose power. Circuits 2b, c, e, g and h will work.

Putting Batteries Together
Learning objectives
- To know that more cells in a circuit cause the bulb to be brighter.
- To know that in a circuit, batteries have to be correctly joined together.
- To know that the ends of a battery are marked + and –.

Ensure that the children understand about recording their prediction prior to testing. Ask the children to work in pairs and organise themselves in sharing the activities (i.e. testing, recording, holding batteries). Circuit tests can be done more than once. If three new 1.5V cells are used, use a 3.5V bulb.

Answers
a= dim, b and c = bright bulb, d–g = bulbs off.

A Flashing Bulb
Learning objectives
- To know how to make a circuit to light a bulb.
- To know how to use a switch to make a bulb flash on and off.

Show children a demonstration model and hide the circuit components behind the picture. Make the bulb flash on and off and ask, 'What is behind the picture to make this happen?' Switches can be ready made for the children or they can make their own from card and tape. Ensure that the bare wire terminals touch when the card is folded closed. Show some switches that do not work and ask why they do not work (e.g. there is tape over wire ends, metal wires miss when card is closed, no metal wire coming out of the wire leads).

Some children may be ready to use more than one bulb in their circuit or may be able to design an alternative switch to make their bulb flash.

Oral work

Discuss circuit components, how wires are joined to bulb holders and how cells are placed into holders. Discuss the shape and structure of a light bulb. Explain: filament, screw thread, etc. Draw pictures of light bulbs and show parts.

Written work

Ask the children to explore how a house light bulb and science bulb are the same. How are they different?

The children could do a survey of the different light switches found in the home (e.g. press – torches, flick or rocker – wall lights, dimmer – wall lights, pull chord – bathroom light). They could also design some switches to make a bulb flash on and off.

ICT

Use CD-ROM to investigate circuits and electricity.

Circuit Problems

You will need
- Cells and holder
- Wires
- Bulb and holder

Key Idea A complete circuit is needed for a bulb to light.

1. Why does the bulb not light up in each of the circuits below? Make the circuits and write your answers.

a. ______________________

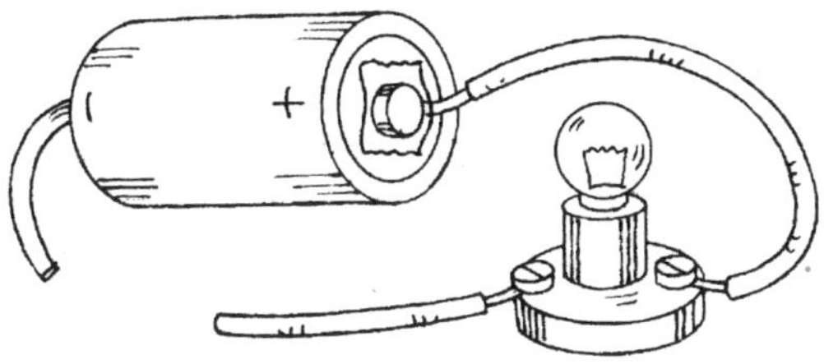

b. ______________________

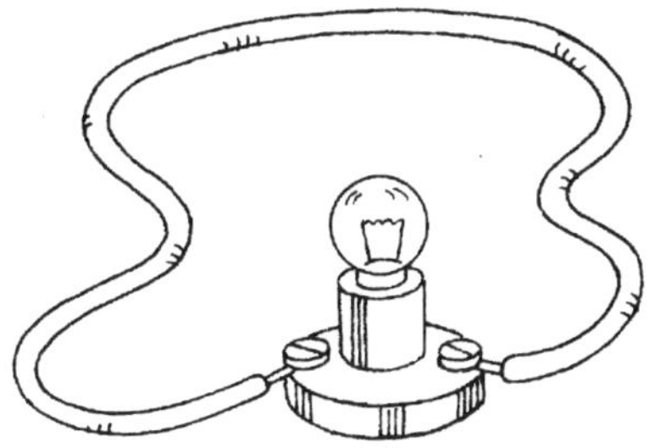

c. ______________________

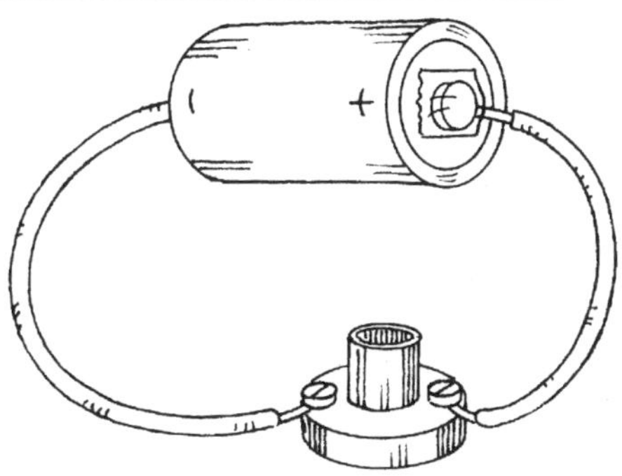

d. ______________________

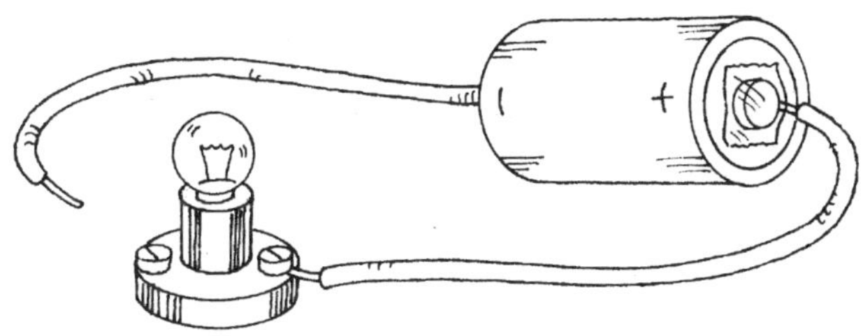

2. Look at the circuits. Which five bulbs will light? ______________

a.

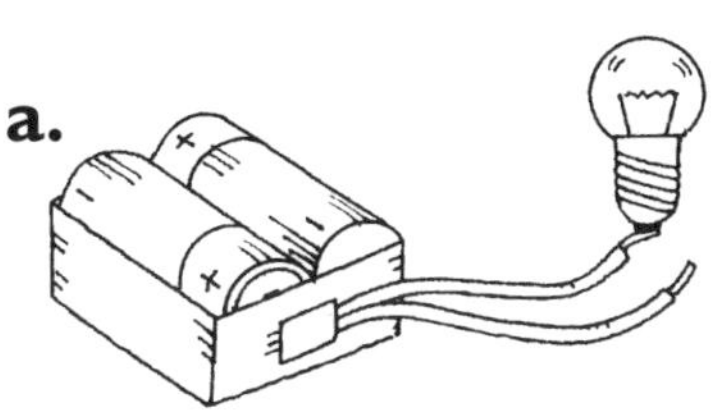

b.

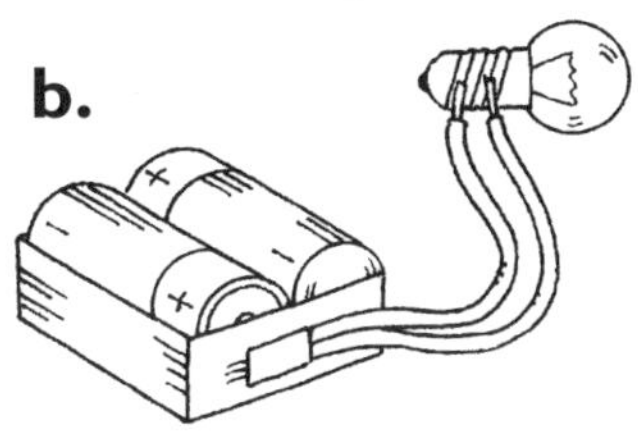

c.

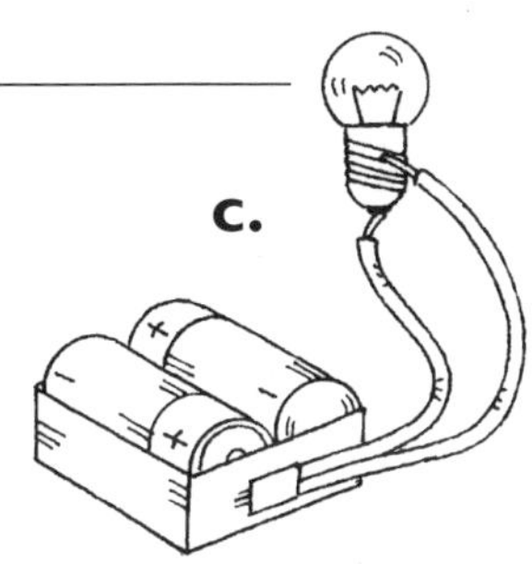

d.

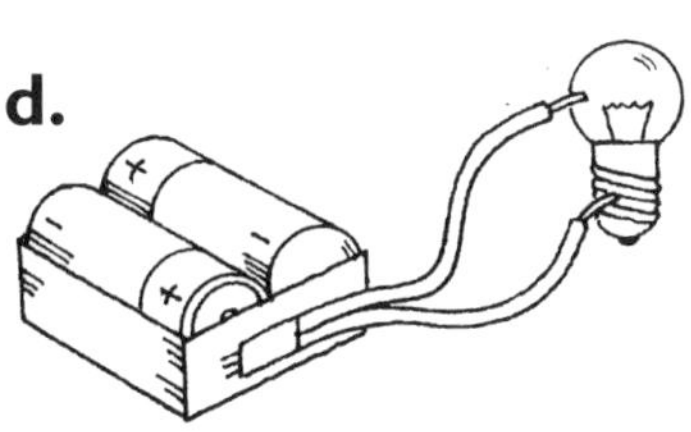

e.

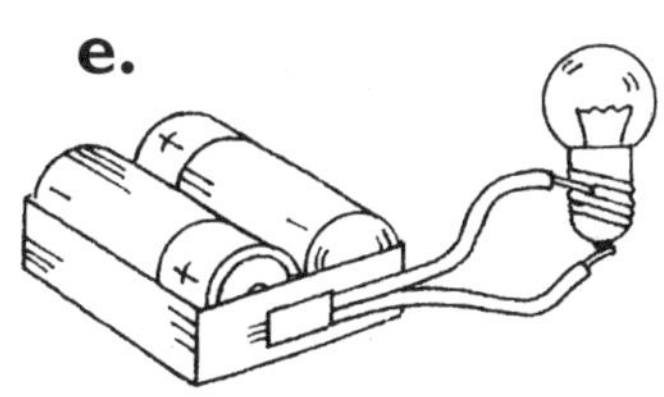

f.

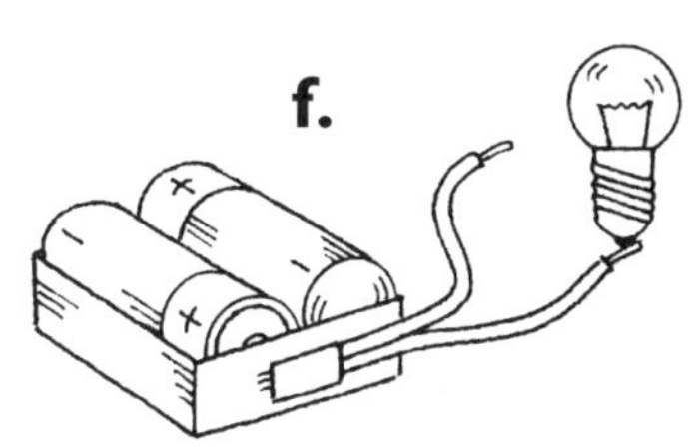

g.

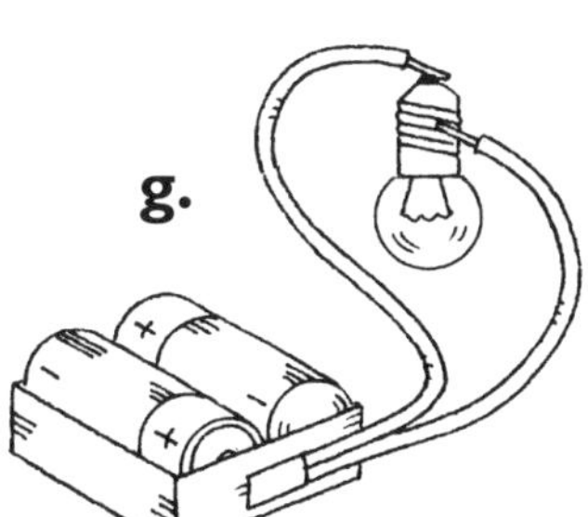

h.

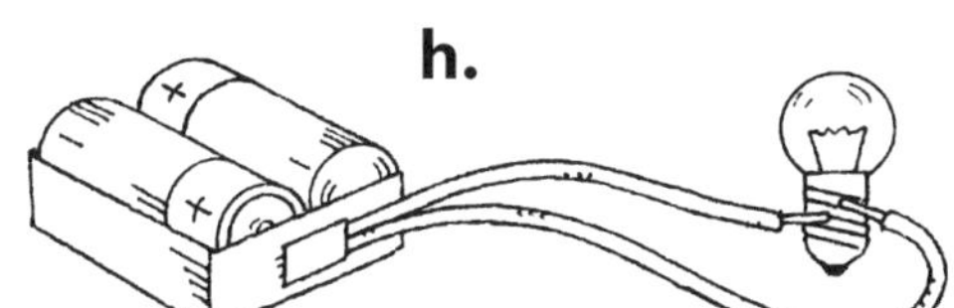

NOW Try the circuits in question 2 to find out if you were right.

Putting Batteries Together

You will need

- Red, yellow and blue crayons
- Three 1.5V cells
- Wires
- Bulb and holder

Key Idea More cells in a circuit cause the bulb to be brighter.

- Look at the circuits and guess whether the bulb in each will glow brightly, dimly or not at all. Look at the colour code and correctly colour each bulb in the 'My guess' column of the table.

How I made my circuit	My guess	What happened
a. 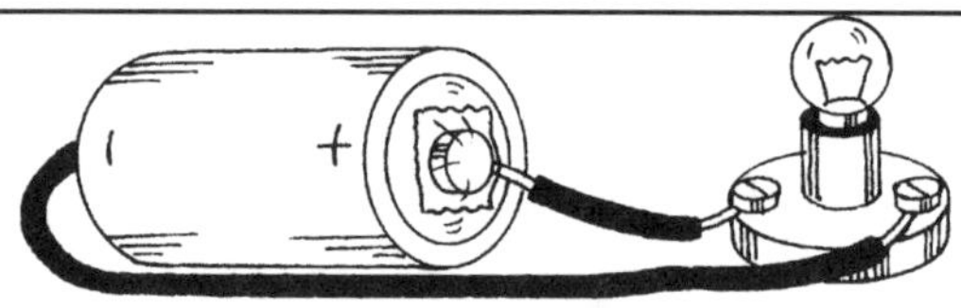		
b. 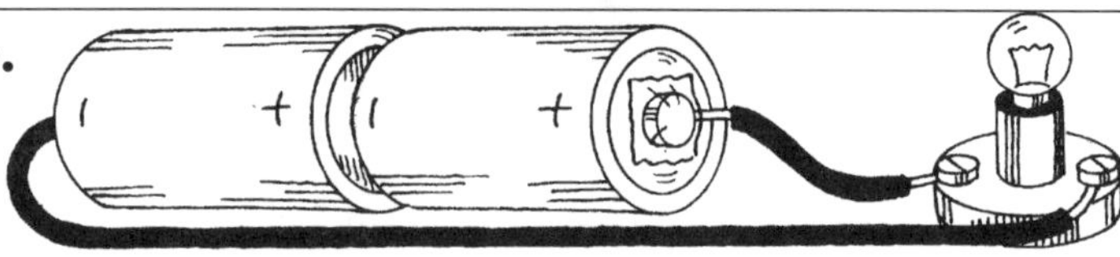		
c. 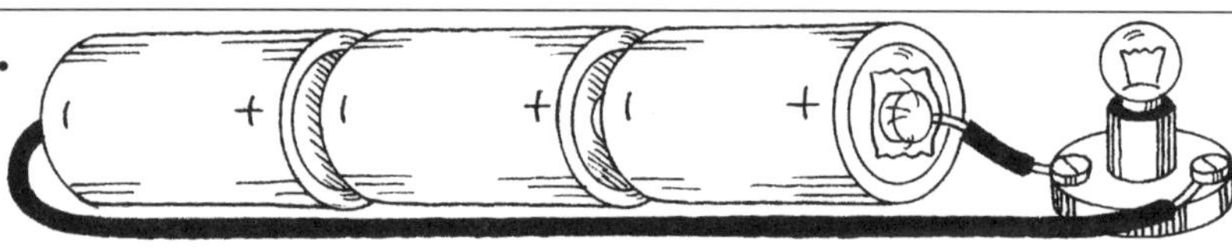		
d. 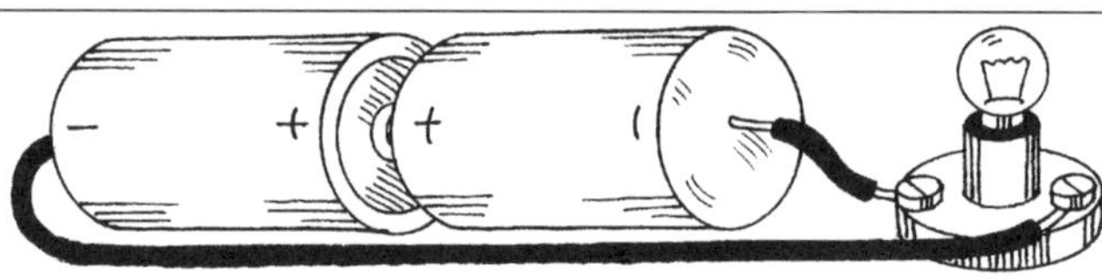		
e. 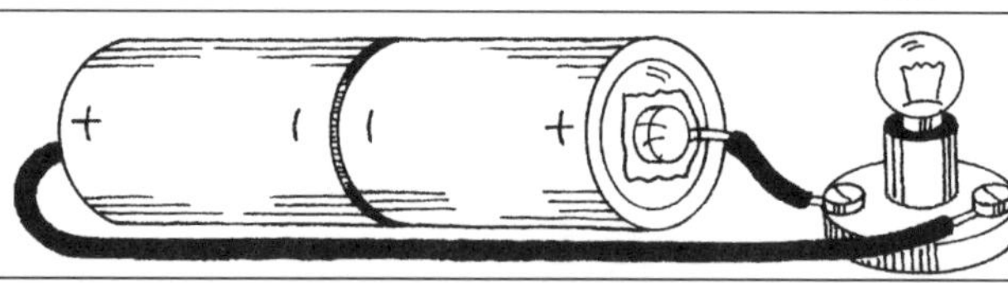		
f. 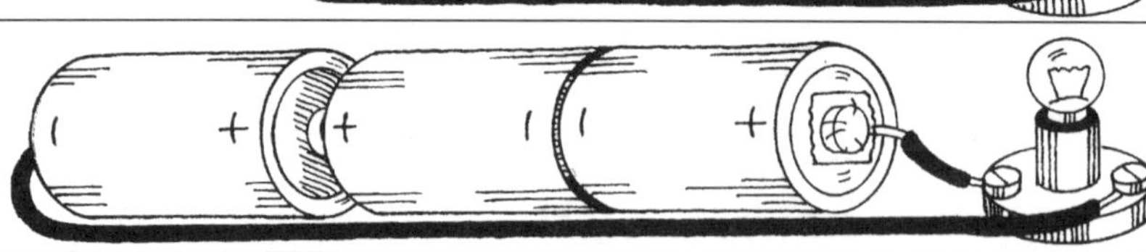		
g. 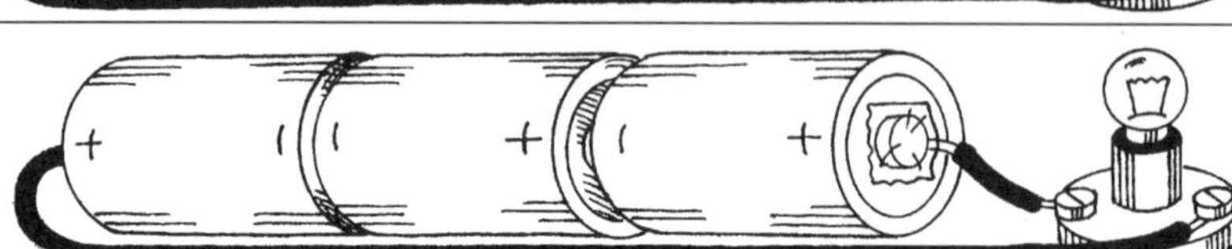		

Colour code

Bright bulb – red | Dim bulb – yellow | Bulb off – blue

NOW Test each of the circuits and colour the bulbs in the 'What happened' column of the table.

A Flashing Bulb

Key Idea A switch can be used to make a bulb flash on and off.

You will need
- Card
- Bulb and holder
- Wires
- Tape
- Cells and holder

- Make a switch and put it into a circuit as below. You could draw a different picture for your bulb if you wish.

Front view

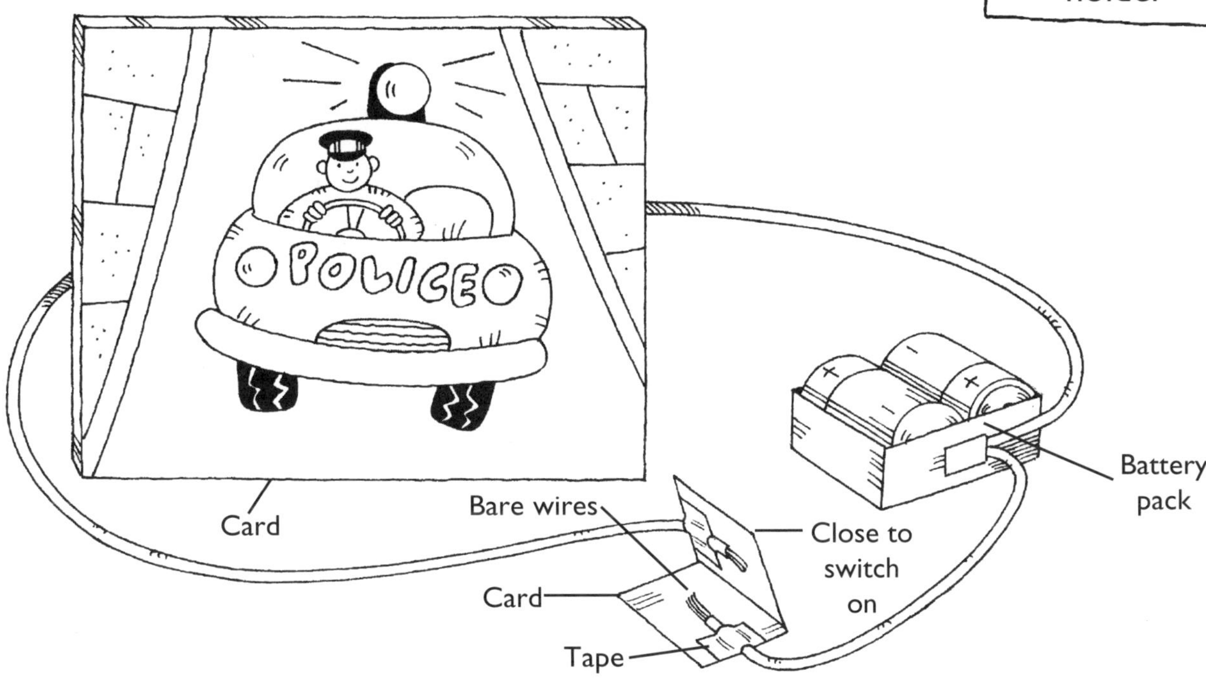

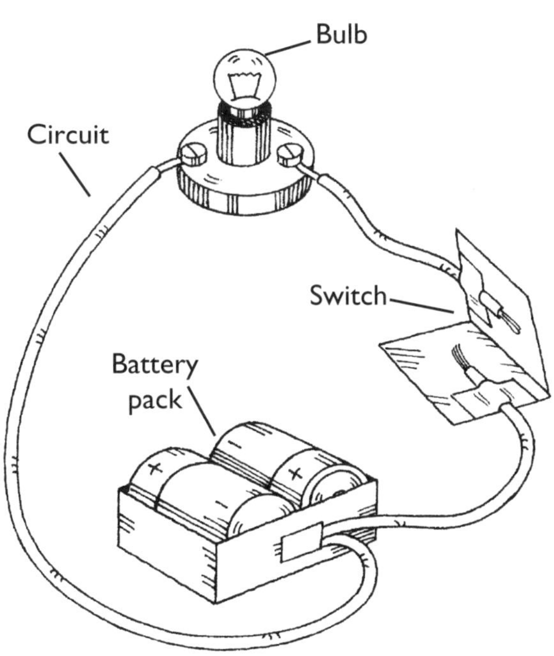

Back view

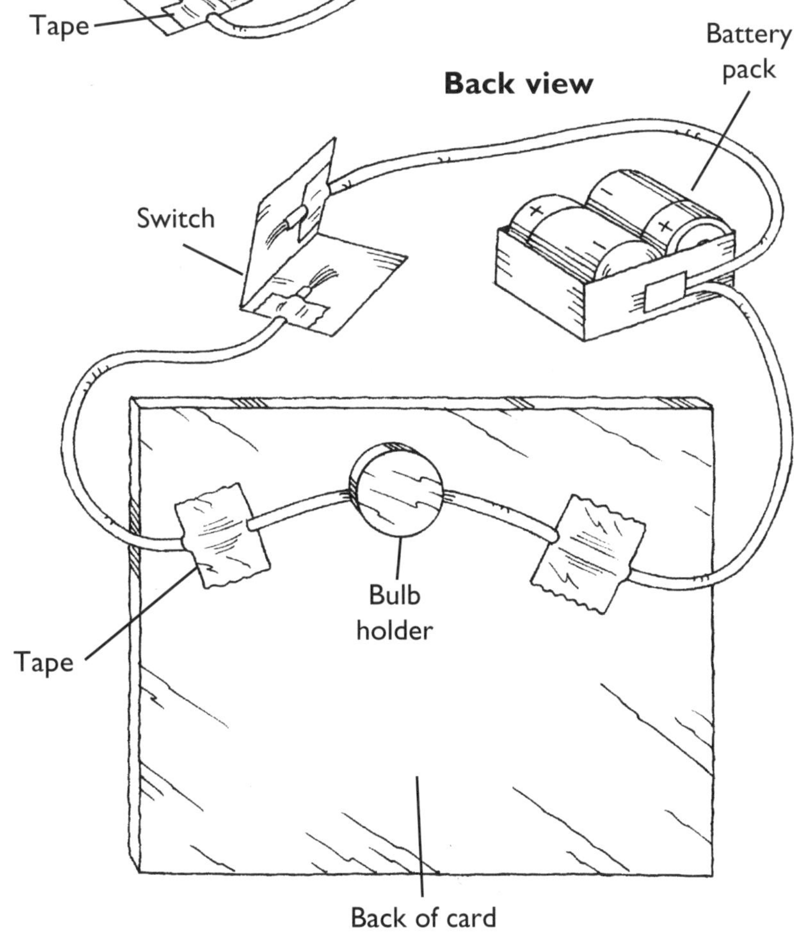

ideas page

Using Electricity

Introduction

Introduce the topic by showing and discussing a simple torch. Ask, 'What is it?', 'What is it used for?', 'How does it work?', 'What is inside it?'. Show a second torch that does not work. Discuss what could be wrong with it (e.g. no batteries, batteries lost their power, batteries wrong way round, bulb broken, etc). Have some spare components available and challenge the children to repair the torch.

Activity pages

Using Electricity
Learning objectives

- To know that some everyday appliances use electricity.

Ask children to sort appliances into groups. They can make up their own groups (e.g. those that use batteries/those that use mains electricity/those that are hand-powered). Appliances could also be grouped as to where they are found around the house or grouped as to what they do: heat, sound, light, movement.

Safety – Mains appliances should only be used if they have been authority-checked and if an earth circuit breaker is used.

Shaky Hand Game
Learning objectives

- To know that electrical devices will not work if there is a break in the circuit.

The activity requires a pre-made model. Show the class how the model works. Follow the circuit from the battery holder along the wire to the buzzer. Explain why the buzzer does not work if the circuit is broken. The buzzer could be replaced with a bulb. Use two 1.5V cells if a 3V buzzer is used and use four 1.5V cells or a 4.5V battery if a 6V buzzer is used.

Circuit Challenge

- To be able to build a complete circuit.
- To be able to build a circuit that uses a switch to control a motor or buzzer.
- To be able to represent a circuit as a drawing.

Challenge 1: Explain that you want the children to make a circuit that operates a motor or a buzzer.

Discuss the components that are available and demonstrate how the wires are joined to the motor and how to join wires together by twisting the metal ends together. Show how batteries are placed into the holder.

Challenge 2: Use a switch in the circuit to control the motor or the buzzer. Children could be given a ready-made switch or make their own switch using card, foil, paperclips, etc.

Oral work

Discuss pictures of things that use electricity. Display some common appliances that use mains electricity and some that use batteries. Why are batteries safer than the mains? What are the dangers of batteries (i.e. swallowing, discharging, can get very hot).

Show and discuss a collection of different sized batteries. Match the battery to the device.

Written work

Carry out a survey showing which appliances are used in the home. Design a safety code for using electricity.

ICT

Use a video to show the dangers of electricity.